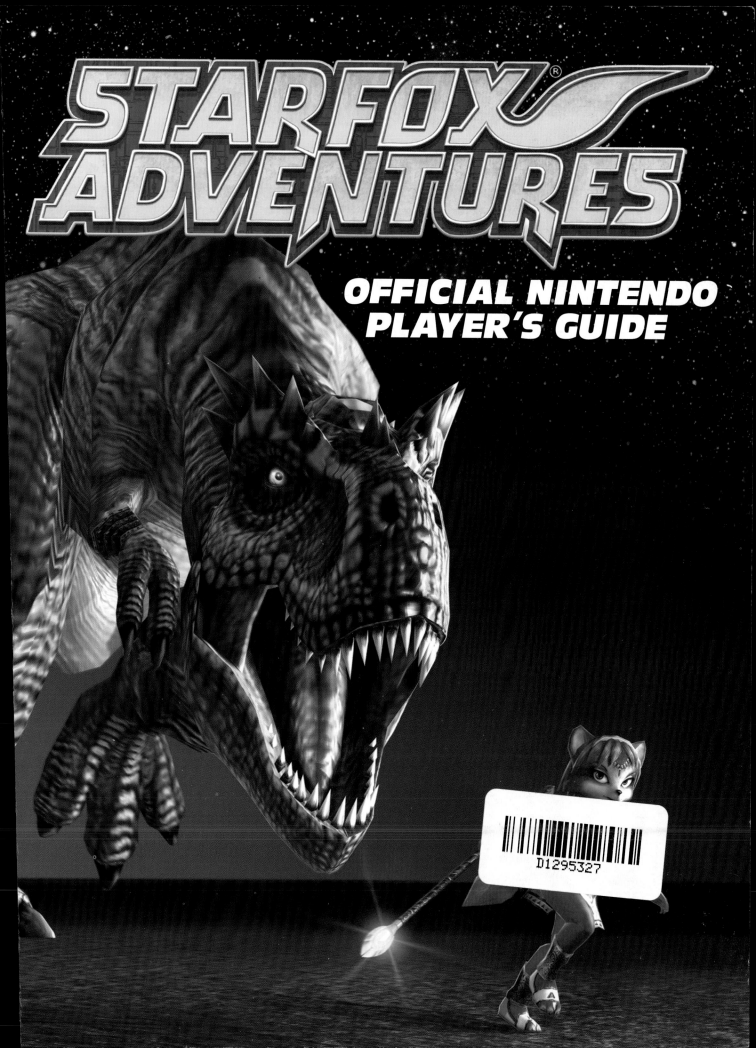

STARFOX ADVENTURES

OFFICIAL NINTENDO PLAYER'S GUIDE

D1295327

TABLE OF CONTENTS

BASICS

PROLOGUE

DINOSAUR PLANET

MEET THE TEAM

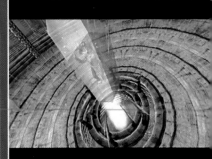

ADVENTURE TOGETHER

Unlike Dinosaur Planet, the Star Fox Team sticks together. Eight years after their triumph over space tyrant Andross, all of the members of the crew of the Great Fox, with the exception of lone eagle Falco Lombardi, are still roaming the Lylat system—looking for adventure and an honest day's pay. While Fox McCloud may do all of the legwork and get most of the glory, the rest of the team offers information, support and a lot of useful tools.

FOX McCLOUD

Star Fox team leader Fox McCloud has spent so much time behind the controls of his Arwing fighter, i hard for him to imagine conflict resolution without a laser blaster and turbo speed, but he'll have to fi more creative solutions to the problems on Dinosaur Planet. Armed with an adventurous spirit and a cunning wit, Fox will begin a long journey to save the planet's distressed inhabitants. He'll find combat clout in the form of Krystal's staff and many useful tools tucked away in the planet's nooks and crannies.

KRYSTAL

She's not officially part of the Star Fox Team, but Krystal does share the team's interest in seeing Gene Scales and his SharpClaw army go down in flames. Roaming the galaxy in search of information abo the demise of her home planet and family, Krystal has been drawn into the fray after answering a distress call from Dinosaur Planet. Following a short adventure in Krazoa Palace, she will be in need of assistance, too. Eventually Fox and Krystal's paths will intersect, after peace returns to the planet.

Was it you that sent the distress signal?

GENERAL PEPPER

General Pepper doesn't fly with the crew, but he does keep in constant contact with them, offering advice and orders. While Fox is roaming Dinosaur Planet and its satellites, he can contact Pepper for information about his current inventory and mission status. The general also keeps track of your progress toward game completion and how many hours you've played.

This mission is about saving the planet, not blowing it up!

SLIPPY

Working behind the scenes, Slippy Toad has kept Rob the Robot and the Arwing running, even in the face of diminishing funds. His current focus is on weapons research and development. When Fox is in need of equipment, he can turn to Slippy. He can also get helpful advice from Slippy in sticky situations.

You've got to go to the Ice Mountain...

PEPPY

Even though his piloting and adventuring days are behind him, Peppy Hare offers moral support and navigational help. When Fox is lost, he can turn to Peppy for directions. Peppy keeps track of all of the maps that Fox purchases from the ThornTail Hollow Store and he loads the maps into the PDA when Fox enters new areas.

A point where pure magic energy is forced up...

ROB

A few too many short circuits have left Rob the Robot a little scatterbrained. In an attempt to deliver Arwing Fuel Cells to Fox, Rob accidentally scattered them all over the planet. Luckily, Fox will be able to find the errant energy units with help from Rob's Fuel Cell Compass.

FALCO

After the Star Fox Team's victory over Andross, Falco Lombardi left the fold and took off for parts unknown. He still keeps up with Fox, but he'll appear only in a cameo near the end of your adventure.

THE DINOSAUR TRIBES

THE PLANET'S POPULATION

Many different types of creatures populate Dinosaur Planet. They are separated into tribes. The tribes don't always get along with each other, but they must join together or the planet will continue to fall apart. The thing that all of the tribes have in common is their opposition to the SharpClaw army of General Scales. Over the course of your adventure, you'll save many dinosaurs from Scales's grasp.

EARTHWALKERS

The self-appointed guardians of Dinosaur Planet preside over Krazoa Palace, and they would rule the Walled City if not for the menacing RedEyes. The EarthWalkers are good friends to have and versatile adventurers. During your Dragon Rock adventure, you will experience the freedom and power of riding on the back of an EarthWalker.

PRINCE TRICKY

After you save Prince Tricky of the EarthWalker Tribe on Ice Mountain, his mother will convince you to take him along for the rest of your journey. While your young charge can be a handful at times, he can also be a big help. Tricky can dig for buried items, scratch through soft dirt to create tunnels, and solve problems with fire. As long as you keep him fed with plenty of Blue GrubTubs, the prince will continue to come to your aid when you need him.

C'mon, Fox, we'll make a great team!

5 3 1 006

SIDEKICK COMMANDS

FIND	STAY	HEEL	FLAME	PLAY

Shortly after you meet Tricky, you will learn about his sidekick commands. With them, you can get Tricky to help you advance your adventure.

HORNTAIL TRIBE

The passive and peaceful members of the ThornTail Tribe occupy Dinosaur Planet's central location—ThornTail Hollow. You will come to the aid of the ThornTails on more than one occasion. Eventually, they will help you, too.

SNOWHORN TRIBE

The massive mammoths who make up the SnowHorn Tribe may not always get along, but they do band together in troubled times. You will find the enormous power of the SnowHorns to be very helpful.

CLOUDRUNNER TRIBE

While the EarthWalkers and the CloudRunners don't see eye-to-eye, you will befriend and get assistance from both tribes. The CloudRunners will be a constant source of help to you once you free them from their fortress prison.

HIGHTOP TRIBE

Even though the HighTops are far from extinct, you will come across precious few of them over the course of your adventures. When you journey to Dragon Rock, you will free a HighTop from prison then ride on the back of the beast over the area's hostile landscape.

LIGHTFOOT TRIBE

The LightFoots have light fingers, too. Some of their prized possessions are involuntary donations from other planet inhabitants. After you pass their tests, they will count you as one of their own.

REDEYE TRIBE

The monstrous carnivores, who have taken over the Walled City, shake the ground with every step. The only way you will be able to defeat them is to take command of an even more powerful ground-shaking force.

SHARPCLAWS

Individual SharpClaw warriors are not very strong, but they have power in numbers. You will encounter SharpClaws in almost every region of the planet and on almost every satellite, including Krazoa Palace. Beware. Some SharpClaws are very large and protected by a lot of armor.

GENERAL SCALES

General Scales will try to convince you that he's not evil—just misunderstood. Don't believe it. Scales is pure evil, from his glaring red eyes to his tough, green skin and razor sharp talons. The general is trying to take control of the planet piece by piece, but you won't let him.

No one can defeat General Scales!

THORNTAIL STORE

Shabunga's store, off ThornTail Hollow's main path, will play a big part in your adventure. Some items that you absolutely need to continue your adventure are available only at the ThornTail Store, and Shabunga will let you have them for a price. At the beginning of your journey, you will be able to afford only a few items. As you collect Scarab Bags and your Scarab-holding capacity increases, so too will your purchasing power.

SHOP AROUND

The ThornTail Store stocks food items, tools and maps. Several items, such as Rock Candy, the FireFly Lantern and the SnowHorn Artifact, are available only at the store and are necessary for the completion of your adventure. Every time you get a larger Scarab Bag, visit the store to find out what new items you can afford.

BARGAIN WITH SHABUNGA

Even though Shabunga lists his prices, he is willing to haggle over the cost of some items. You can make him an offer and see if he'll take it.

FIND LOOSE CHANGE

You'll find Scarabs under a rock in a hidden room on your way to the Scarab game. Others are in baskets. Use a Rocket Boost Pad to reach a ledge that has several Scarab-holding baskets.

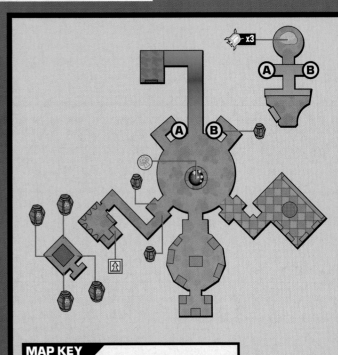

SCRAMBLE FOR SCARABS

In one of the store's remote chambers, Shabunga will challenge you to a Scarab-collection game. He'll throw an armful of Scarabs into the room. If you can catch them all without touching the dark ones within a time limit, you'll earn a prize.

THE WARPSTONE

The animated rock man with the Scottish accent rules over a garden and pond on the upper outskirts of ThornTail Hollow. He may not warm up to you at first, but once you treat him to some Rock Candy, he will reluctantly warp you to some out-of-the-way destinations. He will even offer you a valuable gift as you advance.

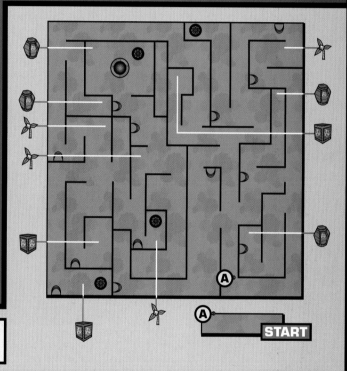

WARP TO ICE MOUNTAIN

You'll encounter the WarpStone early in your adventure. After Queen EarthWalker asks you to save her son, you'll discover that the only way to get to Prince Tricky's location is with help from the WarpStone. A Rock Candy gift will break the ice between the two of you and will prove to be your ticket to Ice Mountain.

WARP TO KRAZOA PALACE

The WarpStone understands the power of the Krazoa Spirits and appreciates how important it is that they be returned to their places in the palace. Whenever you are possessed by a spirit, the WarpStone will be happy to send you to Krazoa Palace.

ENTER THE MAZE

The underground passages under the WarpStone form a maze. Any time you want to pick up gems or life-replenishing items, you can enter the maze and have a look around. Drop tokens in the Token Well there to unlock some cheats.

MAP KEY

 SharpClaw Basket    Magic Plant   SharpClaw Crate

START

KRAZOA SPIRITS

The sacred spirits who protect the magical interests of Dinosaur Planet scattered to the far corners of Dinosaur Planet and its new moons when General Scales and his SharpClaw army took over. In addition to collecting the four SpellStones, you must take all of the Krazoa Spirits back to the palace for the planet to be reformed and for peace to return to the land.

TAKE CONTROL

ARWING OPERATION

Before you can explore Dinosaur Planet and its surrounding moons, you've got to get to your destination. When it comes to flying through debris-packed space zones, the Arwing is your vehicle of choice. You'll zig, zag, dive and climb with pinpoint accuracy as you make your wa around obstacles, shoot down enemy spacecraft and collect preciou Gold Rings.

L AND R BUTTONS

The L and R Buttons allow you to tilt to the left and right. Press them lightly to bank as much as 180 degrees. Press them until they click to make the Arwing spin.

CONTROL STICK

Use the Control Stick to steer the Arwing up, down, left and right. Press Up to descend and press Down to ascend.

Y BUTTON

Tap the Y Button for a brief burst of speed. Press and hold the button for slightly longer speed burst.

X BUTTON

Press the X Button to apply the brakes and reduce your speed.

A BUTTON

The A Button controls the Arwing lasers. Press the button quickly an repeatedly for a steady laser attac

B BUTTON

After you collect a bomb upgrade, can launch it by tapping the B Butt Hit B again when the Bomb is in the to detonate it.

START BUTTON

Press the Start Button to pause the action.

SCREW ATTACK

Press the L or R Button until it clicks into position to initiate a temporary spinning move. A spin protects your ship from laser attacks and allows you to take slightly tighter turns.

SPEED CONTROL

The Arwing advances through space at a steady rate. You can ad your speed slightly by pressing the X and Y Buttons. It takes tim the Y-generated boosting power and X-generated braking powe regenerate, so use the maneuvers sparingly.

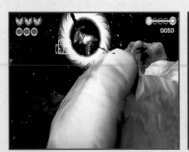

ACCUMULATE POWER AND GOLD

As you fly through space debris, you must keep your eyes open for upgrades and rings. Upgrades make your lasers stronger or give you the ability to release bombs. By accumulating Gold Rings, you can make the force fields around your destination disappear.

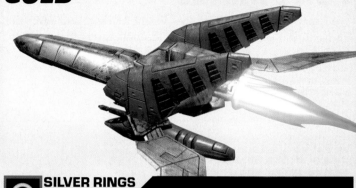

GOLD RINGS

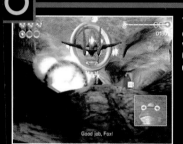

You must collect a certain number of Gold Rings to clear the way to your destination. The number of Gold Rings that you have to collect depends on where you are going.

SILVER RINGS

Silver Rings don't contribute to the destruction of force fields, but they do contribute to your score and energy. Collect them to stay alive longer and to make your way up the High Scores list.

GOLD X RINGS

The centers of some Gold Rings are blocked by obstacles that are marked with an X. Before you can fly through a blocked ring, you must aim for the X and destroy the obstacles.

MOVING RINGS

Some Gold Rings move up and down, or left and right. As you approach a moving ring, watch the way that it moves and try to anticipate where it will be when you get close. You can also use your speed controls to time your approach.

SPECIAL BOXES

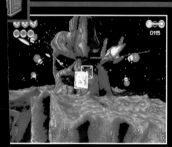

Each box marked with an S holds an upgrade. Fire on boxes to destroy them and reveal the nature of the power-up item.

LASER UPGRADE

Your success in enemy- and asteroid-packed areas depends on the strength of your weapons. Laser upgrades add power to your laser blasts, decreasing the number of times you must hit an obstacle to destroy it.

BOMBS

The best way to clear a large collection of obstacles is with bombs. After you release a bomb, it will shoot out into space and explode, hitting every object in its range with tremendous force. You can make it detonate earlier by tapping the B Button.

MOVING X RINGS

You will occasionally encounter an X-blocked ring that moves. Fire rapidly as you approach the ring to clear away the obstacle and be ready to adjust your speed to catch it as it moves.

FOX FINESSE

You'll control both Krystal and Fox over the course of your adventure. The controls for both characters are identical, except that you won't have a staff when you are in control of Krystal. Move, roll, climb and fight your way to victory.

L BUTTON
Press L to make the camera swing around to the back of your character. Hold L to execute sidestep mode.

CONTROL STICK
Use the Control Stick to move your character, aim projectile weapons and activate combat combo moves.

CONTROL PAD
Press Left and Right on the Control Pad to cycle through the three functions of your PDA.

START BUTTON

Press Start to pause the action and call up your Star Fox Team communication interface.

C STICK
You can use the C Stick to call up your inventory and select items, or to zoom with the Hi-Def Display Device.

R BUTTON

Press and hold the R Button to block or create a defensive force field with your staff.

Z BUTTON
Press the Z Button to toggle in and out of first-person perspective.

X BUTTON

Press the X Button to roll. You can avoid enemies with a roll and make hard landings softer.

Y BUTTON
If you press Y after selecting an entry in your menu, you will assign the selected function to the Y Button. In battle, use the button for staff power attacks.

B BUTTON
The B Button is the cancel button. Use it to put away the staff, close menus and break from battle.

A BUTTON
The A Button is the action button. Use it to attack, activate selected items and talk to other characters.

"A" IS FOR "ACTION"

The A Button initiates several different actions, depending on the situation. If you position your character close to another character, a sign or an object that you can manipulate, a green A Button icon will appear on the screen. Press the A Button to interact with the character or object. The A Button also triggers attacks and activates the selected item or action in your C Stick inventory.

You can initiate the most pressing action with a tap of the A Button. Talk to creatures, hit switches or grab onto objects that you can manipulate.

AUTOMATIC ACTIONS

Fox McCloud is an athletic adventurer with the ability to jump far and climb high. will jump automatically if you steer him over a ledge and he'll climb if you push h up against a climbable surface.

C YOUR INVENTORY

The main function of the C Stick is to call up and cycle through the inventory m Press A to use the selected item or press Y to assign the item to your Y Butto

STICK TO IT

Your first activity while controlling Fox McCloud will be to find Krystal's staff. You can use the versatile tool to fight enemies, activate switches and perform staff upgrade functions.

MASTER STAFF COMBAT

When you engage in combat with adversaries, you can use your staff in several different ways. Press the A Button to swing the staff and hold the Control Stick in one of four directions to initiate a combination attack. By pressing Down while you attack, you can spin the staff and power it up. Press X to roll and stun some enemies with your next attack.

UPGRADE STAFF ABILITIES

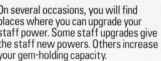

On several occasions, you will find places where you can upgrade your staff power. Some staff upgrades give the staff new powers. Others increase your gem-holding capacity.

FIRE BLASTER

The Fire Blaster is the first staff upgrade that you will find. Use it to shoot blasts of energy at enemies and Fire Blast Switches.

ROCKET BOOST

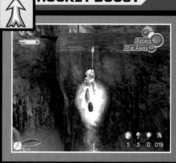

The Rocket Boost propels you up to high ledges and out-of-the-way areas. You can use it only on Rocket Boost Pads.

ICE BLAST

You can extinguish flames and freeze enemies with the freezing mist of the Ice Blast.

GROUND QUAKE

Shake the area around you with a Ground Quake and stun nearby enemies. An advanced Ground Quake upgrade is powerful enough to knock over the bulky members of the RedEye tribe.

PORTAL DEVICE

The special square doors that have circular openings in their centers are called "portals." Once you have the Portal Device, you can use it to insert the staff into a portal's center and make the portal open.

SHARPCLAW DISGUISE

You'll earn the SharpClaw disguise as you explore the SharpClaw-controlled CloudRunner Fortress. Use it to fool SharpClaw guards, carry items that only SharpClaws can carry and initiate actions by standing on SharpClaw pads.

ITEMS AND UPGRADES

FOX'S FINDS

During your struggle to bring the broken pieces of Dinosaur Planet back together, you will accumulate a lot of stuff. Some items will help you stay alive. Some will help you help others. Some will act as keys to locked areas. As you embark on your journey, it pays to know what you should be looking for and what each item can do for you.

ALPINE ROOT

You may not want to eat Alpine Roots yourself, but SnowHorns thrive on them. The best way to get a SnowHorn to do something for you is to feed it a root or two.

BAFOMDAD

The happy, hopping BafomDads revive you and replenish some of your energy after your energy meter has been depleted. Tricky will root out some BafomDads for you. You'll find others in crates and on ledges.

BAFOMDAD HOLDER

For a small fee, you can purchase a BafomDad Holder in the ThornTail Hollow Store. It allows you to have more than one BafomDad in reserve at a time.

BLUE GRUBTUB FUNGUS

EarthWalkers are goofy for GrubTubs. Before you can get Tricky to do anything for you, you must offer him a handful of the mushrooms. You'll find them all over Dinosaur Planet. Stun them with Fire Blaster shots or wait until they are asleep to collect them.

BOMB SPORE PLANT AND BOMB SPORE

When you hit a Bomb Spore Plant with a Fire Blast shot, it explodes, creating a wave of damaging energy and blowing holes in weak walls and soft ground. Some Bomb Spore Plants also spawn Bomb Spores. Cultivate the spores to create plants and blast through rock to caves and hidden areas.

BRIDGE COG

You'll find a collection of Bridge Cogs in the DarkIce Mines area. You'll use them to fix mechanisms that extend bridges across wide gaps.

CLOUDRUNNER FLUTE

Queen CloudRunner has lost track of her children. She'll give you a special flute that will instruct her children to fly to her. You'll use it to gather the princes and princesses in CloudRunner Fortress.

FIREFLY

FireFlies bring light to the FireFly Lantern. After a FireFly burns out, you must put another one into the the lantern. You can purchase them at the store or find them near dark areas.

DINOSAUR HORN

SnowHorns respond to the sound of the Dinosaur Horn. You can use it to call a SnowHorn for a ride and to make your way through a SnowHorn obstacle course.

FIREFLY LANTERN

The FireFly Lantern is required equipment for your adventure in the ancient well. You can purchase it at the ThornTail Store.

DUMBLEDANG TREE AND POD

Tropical DumbleDang Pods grow on tall palm trees. You can knock them to the ground by shaking the trees with your staff. Pick up a pod to replenish a portion of an energy unit.

FROST WEED

If there is something that SnowHorns like more than Alpine Roots, it's Frost Weeds. You'll feed Frost Weeds to Garunda Te, with Tricky's help, in an effort to save the DarkIce Mines GateKeeper from an icy prison in SnowHorn Wastes.

FIRE GEMS

Two Fire Gems act as keys to Ocean Force Point Temple. You'll get one of them from a scheming LightFoot and the other from a statue near the temple entrance.

FUEL BARREL GENERATOR AND BARREL

Fuel Barrels explode when they are exposed to heat or hard landings. You can use their explosive properties to destroy some obstacles. After you use a Fuel Barrel, a nearby Fuel Barrel Generator will create another one.

FIRE WEED

When the ThornTail Hollow Beacons are extinguished by menacing SharpClaws, the dinosaurs will call on you to restore the fire. You'll use Fire Weeds and Tricky's Flame Command to light the beacons.

FUEL CELL

Fuel Cells power the Arwing fighter. You must have a certain number of Fuel Cells to reach each new destination. You'll find the items scattered throughout Dinosaur Planet. Use the Fuel Cell Compass to find the closest one.

GOLD BARS

You'll meet a gold-hungry dinosaur on your first trip to Cape Claw. He'll ask you to dig up four Gold Bars on the beaches. After you return to him with the gold, he'll help you progress on your quest to free Queen CloudRunner.

MOONSEED

You can collect MoonSeeds after you defeat the creatures that pop out of craters in the upper reaches of Moon Mountain Pass. Plant the seeds in planting patches and use Tricky's Flame to make them grow into climbable vines.

HI-DEF DISPLAY DEVICE

Your first-person perspective view will gain new focus when you purchase the Hi-Def Display Device. You must have it during your quest to collect the Sun and Moon Stones on your second visit to the Walled City.

PDA

Fox never leaves his ship without his PDA. You can use it to find Fuel Cells, call up a map of the current area (provided that you have purchased the map from the ThornTail Hollow Store) or get a description of nearby objects.

KEYS

Many inhabitants of Dinosaur Planet, as well as many valuable items, have been locked away in prisons and vaults. You must collect the keys necessary to open locked doors.

POWER KEY

General Scales has cut power to the CloudRunner Fortress wind lifts. You'll get the power key from a BoneHead. Use it to enter the power generator room.

LIGHT GEMS

Three gems give power to the CloudRunner Fortress generator. You must find them in the fortress to restore the power.

PUKPUK EGG

PukPuk Eggs are delicious and good for you. Each egg replenishes a full unit of your energy meter.

MAP

Shabunga sells maps of nearly every location that you will explore. After you purchase the maps, you will find their data in the PDA.

REDEYE TEETH

The Gold and Silver Teeth of the Walled City act as keys to the chamber below the main temple. You'll use them on your way to the RedEye boss battle.

ROCK CANDY

One of the first items that you will purchase from the ThornTail Store is a large, crunchy treat that will put you in the WarpStone's good graces.

Aaaah. A lovely sweetie! Hmmmm...

SCARAB BAGS

As your adventure progresses, you will collect bags that hold more and more Scarabs, increasing the number of items that you can purchase at the store.

But, I've got this for you...

SCARABS

Scarabs are currency on Dinosaur Planet. You can use them to purchase items at the store and to bribe your way into some passages. You'll find them in baskets and under rocks. They scatter when exposed to light. The most valuable Scarabs are the fastest.

SHARPCLAW BASKET

You can pick up and toss small baskets and slash large baskets with your staff. After you break them open, you'll find valuable items inside.

SHARPCLAW CRATE

Some crates block passages and Rocket Pads. Most crates hold useful items, such as PukPuk Eggs. You can break large crates with your staff and pick up small crates while wearing the SharpClaw disguise.

SHARPCLAW ITEMS

SharpClaws carry some items that you can't carry as Fox McCloud. Before you can pick up certain barrels and baskets, you must activate the SharpClaw disguise that you will acquire during your CloudRunner Fortress adventure.

SNOWHORN ARTIFACT

The LightFoots aren't the only characters who take items that don't belong to them. Shabunga acquired a SnowHorn Artifact from the SnowHorn Tribe long ago. You'll need the Large Scarab Bag to carry all of the Scarabs required to purchase it from Shabunga's store.

I don't believe it!

SPELLSTONES

The four SpellStones of Dinosaur Planet help keep the planet together. You must return two SpellStones to Volcano Force Point Temple and two SpellStones to Ocean Force Point Temple to help restore peace to the planet.

STAFF ENERGY GEM AND MAGIC PLANT

Your staff upgrades use energy. You can replenish staff power by collecting gems. They grow on Magic Plants. Cut the plants with your staff and collect the gems.

SUN AND MOON STONES

On your last visit to the Walled City, you will collect the Sun Stone and the Moon Stone in the Sun and Moon Temples. You'll use them to access the Krazoa test warp.

TOKEN WELL

You can buy Cheat Tokens from magic wells scattered throughout Dinosaur Planet and its satellites. Throw them into the well in the Game Well Maze to activate game cheats, such as a Credits-viewing option or a music test.

WHITE GRUBTUB FUNGUS

While Blue GrubTub Fungus is an EarthWalker staple, White GrubTub Fungus has medicinal value. You'll collect six of the mushrooms to help Queen EarthWalker when she is ill. You can find them in the darkness of the ancient well.

TRICKY'S BALL

Tricky is a playful pup of an EarthWalker. When he's bored, he likes to run and chase things. You can buy a ball in the store for him to play with. As you play with him, he'll change colors!

WOODEN COGS

After your first visit to Ocean Force Point Temple, the LightFoot Tribe will take you captive. Once you escape, you'll use three wooden carvings to operate mechanisms that will allow you to explore the village.

USING THE GUIDE

The strategy pages of the guide cover the entire game, organized by area. After the prologue, you'll start in the Dinosaur Planet section, then flip to other sections as the story moves to the planet's satellites. You'll return to the Dinosaur Planet section several times, always turning to the page that follows the last Dinosaur Planet chapter that you read.

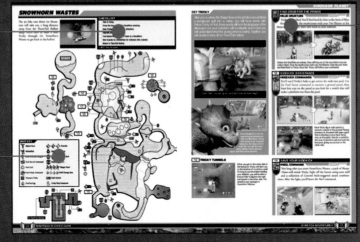

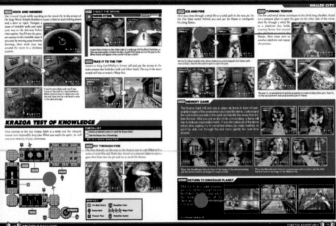

CHECKLIST

Every time the story takes you to another part of Dinosaur Planet or to one of the planet's moons, you'll find a checklist that covers the activities you will participate in as you progress.

MAP KEY

A key accompanies every map. Using symbols, it indicates all of the important objects and items that will be available to you in your current exploration of an area.

MAP

A map details every area and points to items that you can collect using the tools that you have collected. Some maps are shown several times. The item placements on the maps are always updated to show the locations of obtainable items.

ICON

Item, upgrade and sidekick command icons accompany tips that explain situations where you can use the pictured tool to advance.

NUMBERED TIP

1 Tips are numbered to reflect their logical place in the game's progression. You'll find a quick description of each ti from first to last, in the Tip Index the end of the guide.

TRAVEL TIME

STOP When you reach the en of a section, you'll see "Stop" sign and a page number in cating where you should go next continue the adventure.

PROLOGUE

A young woman looking for answers about past events finds herself in the middle a developing struggle between the SharpClaw army of General Scales and the inhabitants of Dinosaur Planet. The adventure begins with Krystal on the back of a CloudRunner, battling Scales's flying ship, and it continues after Krystal finds herself in a crystal prison in Krazoa Palace.

THE ADVENTURES BEGIN

While on a mission to uncover the truth about the deaths of her parents, a young woman finds herself in the middle of an epic struggle. The story of Dinosaur Planet begins.

I received a garbled distress signal.

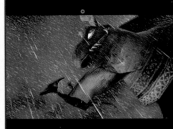

CHECKLIST

- [ ] Battle General Scales's flying ship.
- [ ] Collect the Krazoa Palace Key and confront General Scales.
- [ ] Fly to Krazoa Palace, open a door and break through boxes.
- [ ] Use a Fuel Barrel to break into the building.
- [ ] Talk to the EarthWalkers.
- [ ] Warp to Krazoa Shrine.
- [ ] Take the Krazoa Test of Observation.
- [ ] Collect, then release, the Krazoa Spirit.

• NEXT: Fly to Dinosaur Planet

FIGHT THE FLYING SHIP

Controlling Krystal on the back of a CloudRunner, you will find yourself behind a flying ship that has a huge propeller and aft-firing guns. Fire at the guns until they catch fire, then concentrate on the propeller. After the propeller is gone, the guns will recharge. Knock them out again, then hit the figurehead when the ship turns to face you.

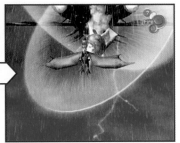

Fire on the guns and the propeller of the massive ship and fly out of the way of its shots. You should be able to do a lot of damage with little effort.

After the guns are repaired, hit them again. With its guns finally disabled for good, the ship will turn around and charge. Concentrate your fire on the fireball-spitting dragon figurehead.

CLUES AND A KEY

◀ KRAZOA PALACE KEY

Step onto the deck of the ship and make your way up to a bird in a cage. After you exchange a few words with the bird, he will open the doors to the cargo compartment. Go below deck to collect the Krazoa Palace Key.

GENERAL ALERT

Ruler, tyrant and dictator of Dinosaur Planet.

After you return to the upper deck, you'll encounter nasty General Scales. He'll let you know about the hardships that he has brought to the creatures of Dinosaur Planet, then kick you off the failing ship. Luckily, your CloudRunner will be there to catch you.

OPEN A DOOR, FIND A TOOL
◄FUEL BARREL

Your CloudRunner will take you to Krazoa Palace. Use the Krazoa Palace Key to open the door to a storage area and pick up a Fuel Barrel. You can use the barrel to destroy blocking boxes or enemies. After you toss the barrel, another one will appear on the nearby barrel generator.

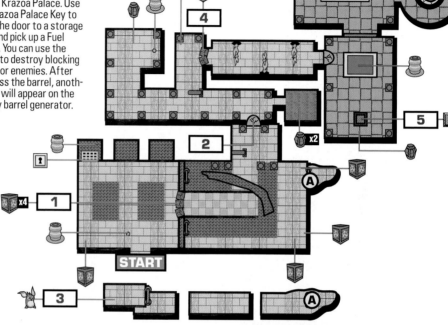

P KEY

- **BafomDad**
- **Fuel Barrel**
- **Fuel Barrel Generator**
- **SharpClaw Crate**
- **Pressure Plate**
- **Release Krazoa Spirit**
- **SharpClaw Basket**

START

HEART HELP
◄PUKPUK EGG

You'll find a dinosaur delicacy inside the first crates that you destroy with an explosive barrel. Each PukPuk Egg regenerates a full section of your energy meter.

These are tasty PUKPUK EGGS...a SharpClaw delicacy!

ID AIRBORNE ENEMIES

The creatures that hover over the open deck of Krazoa Palace kick out their tentacles as they spin and deliver damaging blows. You can destroy the creatures with exploding barrels or simply avoid them altogether as you explore the area.

POWER PRODUCTION
◄FUEL BARREL GENERATOR

As soon as you use a Fuel Barrel, the Fuel Barrel Generator on the main deck will produce another one. Be sure to pick up a barrel from the generator before you make your way down the ramp.

Each time you use a barrel, another will be...

ADDED ENERGY
◄DUMBLEDANG POD

You have collected a DUMBLEDANG POD.

In addition to PukPuk Eggs, you will find energy-restoring DumbleDang Pods. They're not quite as powerful as the eggs, but every little bit helps.

INFO AND ADVICE

The King EarthWalker sent us to protect...

The Krazoa Palace EarthWalkers will tell you about the trials of the planet's dinosaurs and give you helpful information about the game controls. Take the time to talk to every one of them.

3 | ENERGY IN RESERVE

◄BAFOMDAD

Climb down the ladder on the edge of the deck, jump over several wide gaps and climb up another ladder—you'll find a BafomDad. If you lose all of your energy, the BafomDad will revive you.

5 | DESTROY THE DOOR

You'll find a Fuel Barrel Generator around the corner from where you found the first interior barrel. Pick up a barrel and take it with you as you run down the flame-filled hall, then destroy the door at the end.

Grab a barrel from the generator, enter the long hall, avoid the flame jets and destroy the weakened door. Place a barrel on a plate in the next area to open a door.

2 | BRING A BARREL BELOW

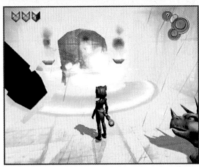

As you explore the lower are the Krazoa Palace deck, you discover a cracked wall. Coll barrel from the generator, c down the ramp and toss it in direction of the cracked wall You'll blow open an entrance the palace interior.

4 | CLEAR AWAY THE CRATES

You'll discover another barrel and blocking crates inside the palace. Toss the b at the crates to clear the way.

6 | DINOSAUR DIALOGUE

The EarthWalker at the entrance to the Krazoa Palace Shr will fill you in on the struggles of the dinosaurs and ope door to a Krazoa Shrine warp. If you can show that you are a worthy adventurer in a Krazoa Spirit test, you will free one of the spirits and begin the task of mending the wounds that General Scales has opened.

The Krazoa... Need your help... They are dying...

LIFEFORCE FOUND

your way to the Krazoa Spirit, you will encounter several obstacles.
first obstacle is a Life-Force Door, which is powered by the enemy
the room. If you destroy the enemy, you'll destroy the door.

ss the pit to the barrel and the Life-Force Door, then toss the barrel at the
ny in the pit. A direct hit will make both the enemy and the door disappear.

APPLY PRESSURE

en you stand on the pressure plate in the second long chamber, the
at the other end will open. You can put a barrel on the plate to
it open or just make a run for it.

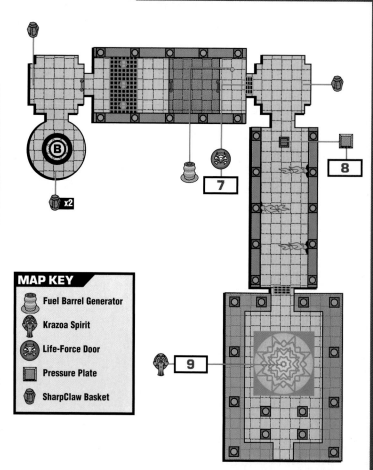

MAP KEY

	Fuel Barrel Generator
	Krazoa Spirit
	Life-Force Door
	Pressure Plate
	SharpClaw Basket

BASKET WATCHING

hen you reach the Krazoa Spirit, it will put your observa-
nal skills to the test. You'll pass the Krazoa Test of Observa-
on if you can find the spirit in a collection of moving baskets.

The Krazoa Spirit will fly into a basket, then the baskets will move. After they stop moving, you must touch the spirit's basket. You must complete the exercise three times in a row to pass the test.

10 RELEASE THE SPIRIT

The Krazoa Spirit will possess you after you pass the test. Return to the entrance to the shrine and take a rising platform up to a new area. You will release the spirit, and Krystal will become a prisoner of the palace.

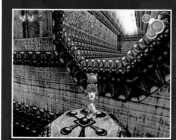 

AM STAR FOX TO THE RESCUE

ith Krystal encased in a glass prison, the story turns
Fox McCloud and his crew. General Pepper clues the
w in on the problems that face Dinosaur Planet.
veral sections of the planet have broken away from
e main sphere. The general tells Fox to go to the
net and investigate the situation. The inhabitants of
e planet need assistance, and the adventuring Fox
n provide a helping paw.

You are approaching Dinosaur Planet...   As you will see, chunks of the planet...

FLY TO DINOSAUR PLANET

FLY THROUGH 1 GOLD RING TO REACH DINOSAUR PLANET

START

A

1

A

END

L

4

B

2

3

B

MAP KEY

B Bomb

L Laser Upgrade

○ Gold Ring

○ Silver Ring

CLEAR THE WAY

You can destroy each small rock with a few blaster shots and each mine with a single shot. Target the obstacles in your path and blow them away.

1 FANCY FLYING

You'll find the second Gold Ring and a bomb power-up in a cloud of small aste[r]oids. Immediately after you collect the ring, dive down and to the right to gra[b] the bomb.

2 RINGS IN A ROW

Good job, Fox!

Watch out for mines!

In the middle of your flight, you will find several Gold Rings, one following the next. As soon as you collect a ring, another one will be in your sights. Grab them both and keep going.

3 TWO CLOSE

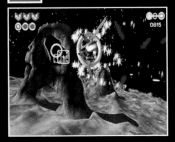

The sixth and seventh Gold Rings are practically on top of each other. Grab the sixth one, veer left and head for th[e] seventh.

4 FIGHT FIRE WITH FIRE

The final Gold Ring is among a large group of mines and enemy ships. Use a [a] bomb to destroy the ships as you clos[e] in on them, then collect the final ring with ease.

DINOSAUR PLANET

hile you will have many adventures on Dinosaur Planet's oons, the planet proper will serve as the hub for your long est to collect the SpellStones and to put them in their places. e main planet will be your source for Fuel Cells and a large col- ction of helpful items, and the inhabitants will provide you th tons of useful information.

THORNTAIL HOLLOW

Fox McCloud's quest to bring the broken pieces of Dinosaur Planet back together begins in ThornTail Hollow, home of the peaceful ThornTail tribe and Queen EarthWalker. As you explore the planet and its errant satellites, you will return to ThornTail Hollow several times to get information from the queen and items from Shabunga's ThornTail store. You'll also use the massive WarpStone to travel to special areas, such as Krazoa Palace. After you bring the Arwing in for a landing for your first visit to the hollow, General Pepper will clue you in on how to communicate with the Star Fox team from the planet's surface.

CHECKLIST

- [ ] Collect Krystal's Staff.
- [ ] Fight SharpClaw attackers and get the Fire Blaster staff upgrade.
- [ ] Talk to the Queen of the EarthWalkers and set out to rescue Prince Tricky.
- [ ] Use Bomb Spores to blast through weak walls.
- [ ] Collect Scarabs to purchase a ThornTail Hollow Map and Rock Candy.
- [ ] Give the Rock Candy to the WarpStone.

• NEXT: Warp to Ice Mountain

TALK TO THE TRIBE

Whenever you arrive in a foreign land, it pays to get advice fr the natives. You'll find large—but friendly—dinosaurs both sides of the river. They'll give you clues about what to and do as you explore ThornTail Hollow.

And don't forget, you're looking for the Queen EarthWalker.

The flight to ThornTail Hollow may be bumpy, but you will have a smooth landing. Once you're on the surface, General Pepper will give you tips on how to contact the team.

They have taken the Queen EarthWalker and locked ..

1 SEARCH FOR THE STAFF

In her battle with General Scales's airship, Krystal dropped her staff into the atmosphere of Dinosaur Planet. It landed in a flower patch in ThornTail Hollow. As adventurer Fox McCloud, you can find the staff and use it to explore the world.

After you pull the staff from the ground, Krystal's voice will tell you about using the staff as a weapon and a tool. As you explore Dinosaur Planet and its new moons, you will discover staff upgrades that give the weapon new powers, such as the ability to fire projectiles and release a freezing mist.

MAP KEY

Bomb Spore Planting Patch

Bomb Spore Plant

DumbleDang Tree

Fire Blast Switch

Fire Blaster Staff Upgrade

Fuel Cell

Map

Rock Candy

Scarabs

SharpClaw Basket

SharpClaw Crate

Magic Plant

Staff Energy Gem

Staff Switch

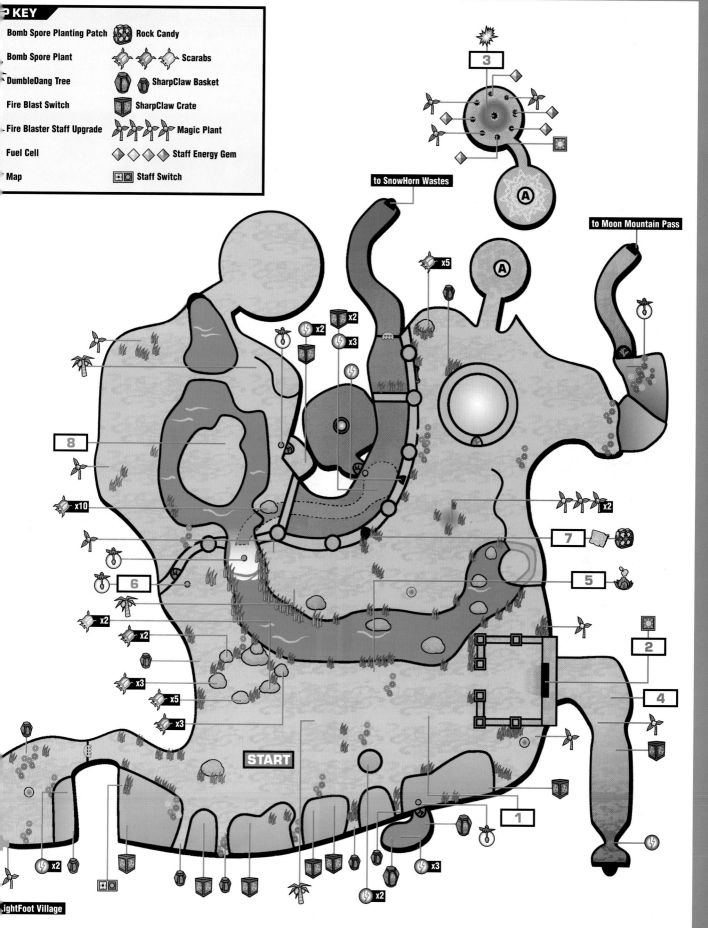

to SnowHorn Wastes

to Moon Mountain Pass

START

LightFoot Village

2 | TAKE ON ATTACKERS

As you approach the home of Queen EarthWalker, four SharpClaws will emerge from the building and your first battle will begin. Press the A Button rapidly to lash out at the enemies with the staff and use the Control Stick to pull off combination attacks. After you defeat the SharpClaws, a Fire Blast Switch will appear above the door.

3 | STAFF UPGRADE

◀ FIRE BLASTER

Your victory against the SharpClaws will open a tunnel entrance on the other side of the river. Explore the tunnel and find the first staff upgrade. It will give you the power to fire blasts of energy at enemies and Fire Blast Switches.

Pull up a rock from the floor of the cave with your staff, then drop into a hole. You'll reach an underground chamber that holds the Fire Blaster staff upgrade and several staff energy gems. A gate blocks the chamber's exit. Hit the Fire Blast Switch with a blast of energy. The switch will change from red to green and the gate will rise.

5 | POWERFUL PLANT

◀ BOMB SPORE PLANT

You'll find a Bomb Spore plant near the Arwing's landing site. If you hit the plant with the power of your Fire Blaster, the plant will explode, creating a damaging wave of energy, and three Bomb Spores will fly into the air. Seconds later, the plant will regenerate.

ENERGY GROWS

◀ STAFF ENERGY GEM

Staff energy gems grow on trees. You'll find a group of plants near the river. Hack them with your staff and collect gems. The gems will fill your staff power meter, giving fu the Fire Blaster.

You picked up a STAFF ENERGY GEM!

4 | CONVERSE WITH THE QUEEN

Return to the place where you fought the SharpClaws and the Fire Blast Switch with a shot of energy. The door will op giving you access to Queen EarthWalker. She will fill y in on the plight of the dinosaurs and ask you to save her son, Prince Tricky, on Ice Mountain. Your next step will be to use the Warp-Stone to reach the icy area. A ThornTail will clear the way to the WarpStone.

- Dino Talk -   - Dino Call -

PLANT A SEED

◀ BOMB SPORE

The Bomb Spores that fly out of an exploding Bomb S Plant are useful tools. You can plant a spore in a Bomb S Planting Patch to create a new explosive plant quickly. You'l several patches in ThornTail Hollow.

Collect floating Bomb Spores after you fire on the hollow's regenerating Bomb Spore plant, then seek out Bomb Spore Planting Patches to plant spores and create new explosive plants.

HAVE A BLAST

Bomb Spore Planting Patches are close to cracked walls. When
reate a Bomb Spore plant with a spore then hit the plant with a
Blast, the resulting explosion will create an opening in the wall.

a Bomb Spore in a Bomb Spore Planting Patch, then fire on the new plant. The
sion will blast open a cracked wall and give you access to a new area. One of
eas that you can blast into is the WarpStone's garden.

CASH ADVANCEMENT
◀ SCARABS

The citizens of Dinosaur Planet use Scarabs as currency. You
can find the valuable bugs under rocks and in baskets. At the
eginning of your adventure, you can hold only 10 Scarabs at one
me. After you collect the Scarab Bag, you'll be able to hold more.

Scarabs hide under boulders and in baskets. You can prop up a boulder with your staff. Press the A Button quickly and repeatedly for a powerful lift. When the Scarabs scatter, drop the rock and go after them. If you want to get a Scarab from a basket, lift the basket and smash it to the ground.

UP POWER

find several Fuel Cells by breaking
aves with the explosive power of
Spore plants. Check out the maps
guide for the locations of all hidden
ells and consult the Fuel Cell Com-
on your PDA for directions to the
cell.

On your way to the WarpStone's garden, you'll discover a Bomb Spore Planting Patch under the waterfall. Plant a spore, then hit the new plant with a Fire Blast. The resulting explosion will give you access to a tunnel where you will find several Fuel Cells.

TALK TO THE ROCK

After you blast into the WarpStone's garden, you'll find the massive rock man on a small island. Hop onto the island and talk to the WarpStone. He'll help you if you bring him a treat.

Nobody ever brings me gifts anymore!

FOX NEEDS FUEL
◀ FUEL CELLS

You'll need Fuel Cells to fly the Arwing to the Dinosaur Planet satellites. The cells are scattered throughout many areas of the planet, including ThornTail Hollow. Seek them out.

Fox automatically leaps when you run past the edge of a ledge. When you're exploring the ledges that line the southern rock wall, have Fox leap to the tall rock that holds Fuel Cells. He'll grab onto the side and climb up.

It always pays to have a few Bomb Spores on hand. While you're exploring the ledges that line the wall close to the queen's home, you'll find a Bomb Spore Planting Patch. Plant a spore there and blast the plant for access into a cave. You'll find Fuel Cells inside.

7 | STOCK UP AT THE STORE

Shabunga's ThornTail Store is in a series of underground chambers, across the river from the Arwing's landing site. When you step into the store for the first time, Shabunga will greet you and give you a quick tour. The shopkeeper sells a wide variety of items, including food and maps. Even though you can bargain with Shabunga, you won't have enough Scarabs to buy many of the items in the store on your first visit. Your Scarab-holding capacity will increase later. Search Shabunga's store for a Scarab-collecting game.

When you pick up an item in the store, Shabunga will give you an initial price. You can raise or lower the amount that you are willing to pay by pressing Up and Down on the Control Stick. Press A to submit your offer.

Magical sparks float from the well in the ThornTail Store lobby. A creature in the well will give you a Cheat Token if you toss enough Scarabs into the water. Come back when you have 20 Scarabs.

 See page 8 for more information about the ThornTail Store

KNOW YOUR WAY AROUND
◄THORNTAIL HOLLOW MAP

The ThornTail Store carries a wide selection of maps. After you buy a map, turn on your PDA and use the Control Stick to cycle to the map. Once you're outside, the ThornTail Hollow map will appear on the display.

Among the many maps that Shabunga sells are parchments that lay out ThornTail Hollow and SnowHorn Wastes. You can try to bargain with the lizard, but the maps are a good deal at any price.

A ROCK FOR THE ROCK MAN
◄ROCK CANDY

The ThornTail Store chamber that feeds off the center passage holds tools, such as and FireFly Lantern and Hi-Def Display Device. The most useful tool that you can afford early on is a chunk of Rock Candy, a perfect gift for the WarpStone.

8 | GET A LIFT

Return to the WarpStone with Rock Candy. When you give sweet to the massive creature, he will reluctantly offer to he His three warp options are Ice Mountain, the Game Well M and Krazoa Palace. Since Prince Tricky is on Ice Mounta that's where you should go. After you press Left on the Control Stick to select Ice Mountain, the WarpStone will take Fox into his hand and send the adventurer warping to the new location.

The WarpStone's middle option is the Game Well Maze, a minigame are where you can unlock cheats. The left option will take you to Ice Mountain, where you'll find Prince Tricky.

See page 9 for more information about the Maze

E MOUNTAIN

SharpClaws are holding Prince Tricky captive in a small encamp-
t on Ice Mountain. You must fight off the guards and find a way
ach the Prince, then guide your young charge back to ThornTail
ow.

CHECKLIST

☐ Destroy a barrier and defeat SharpClaw guards.
☐ Blast a switch to open the door to Tricky's cell.
☐ Race SharpClaws on jet bikes to rescue the fleeing prince.

• NEXT: Continue on to SnowHorn Wastes

P KEY

Bomb Spore Planting Patch

Token Well

Fire Blast Switch

Fuel Barrel Generator

Fuel Cell

Scarabs

SharpClaw Crate

Magic Plant

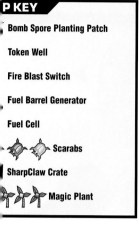
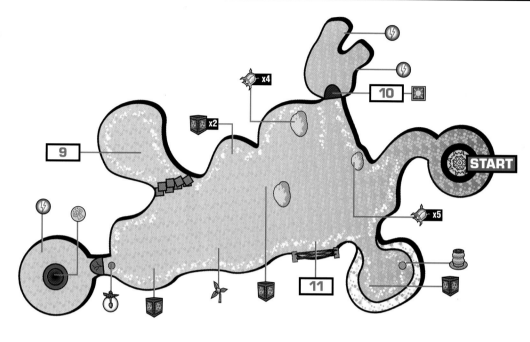

BLAST BOXES, BEAT BADDIES

ge stack of boxes blocks the path to a SharpClaw hangout. Pick
ticking powder keg and toss it at the boxes to blow away the bar-
A pair of SharpClaw guards wait for you on the other side.

10 PASSAGE TO THE PRINCE

Your victory over the guards will cause a Fire Blast Switch to appear
above the door to Prince Tricky's cell. After you enter the cell, Tricky
will escape and his guards will give chase on jet bikes.

RET CAVE

you carried a Bomb Spore into the Ice Mountain area, you're
luck. You can blast your way into a cave on the west end that
lds a single Fuel Cell and a well.

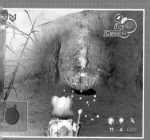

11 HIT THE SLOPES

The SharpClaws will leave behind an extra jet bike. You'll jump
onto the bike and race against the SharpClaws down the Ice
Mountain slope. Press and hold the A Button to accelerate, watch
out for obstacles and cut corners to gain ground on the guards.

SNOWHORN WASTES

The jet bike race down Ice Mountain will take you a long distance away from the ThornTail Hollow warp. You'll have to hoof it with Tricky through the SnowHorn Wastes to get back to the hollow.

CHECKLIST

- [ ] Talk to Tricky.
- [ ] Cross the lava pool to the SnowHorn clearing.
- [ ] Save Tricky from SharpClaw attackers.
- [ ] Upgrade your staff.
- [ ] Find Alpine Roots and feed them to a SnowHorn.
- [ ] Give Scarabs to a BribeClaw for entrance into a tunnel.
- [ ] Return to ThornTail Hollow.

• NEXT: Help the queen

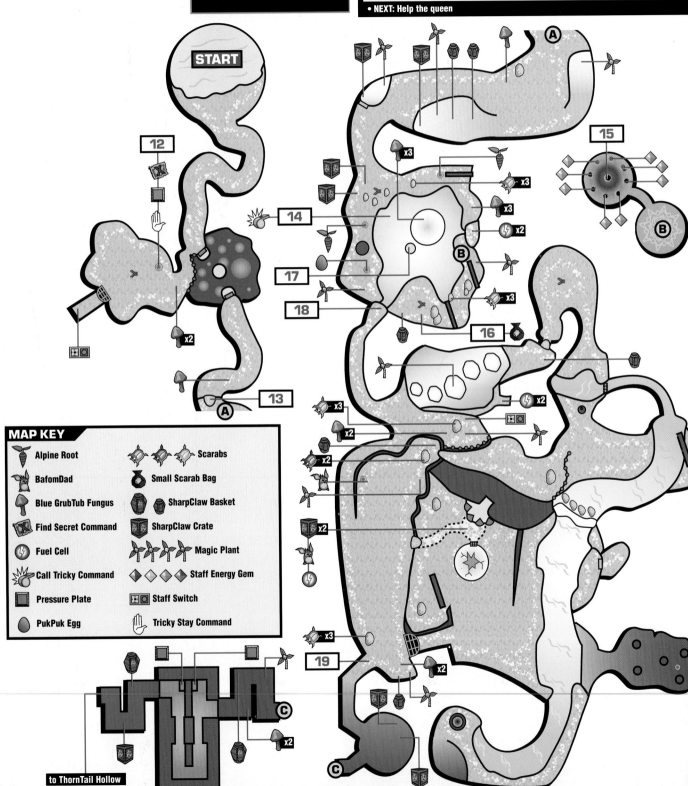

MAP KEY

Alpine Root		Scarabs	
BafomDad		Small Scarab Bag	
Blue GrubTub Fungus		SharpClaw Basket	
Find Secret Command		SharpClaw Crate	
Fuel Cell		Magic Plant	
Call Tricky Command		Staff Energy Gem	
Pressure Plate		Staff Switch	
PukPuk Egg		Tricky Stay Command	

TRICKY

fter you overtake the SharpClaws in the jet bike race and take
spectacular spill into a ravine, you will have words with
rince Tricky. At first, those words will be in the language of the
nosaurs, but your translator will eventually kick in and you
ill understand what the young prince is saying. Together, you
ill decide to take off for ThornTail Hollow.

(Dino Talk)...hot spring or you'd be frozen by now (laugh).

Even though he is not an experienced adventurer, like Fox McCloud, Tricky will prove to be a helpful sidekick. As long as he is well fed, he can discover many hidden items and passages and help solve puzzles.

TRICKY TUNNELS

After you get to the other side of the lava pool, Tricky will alert you to the location of a crack in a wall. As long as you have been feeding your sidekick, you will be able to instruct him to dig into the wall and tunnel to the other side. The tunnel is your passage to SnowHorn Wastes.

FIND GRUB FOR THE PRINCE
◄BLUE GRUBTUBS

Tricky is famished. You'll find food for him in the form of Blue GrubTubs. Stun the mushrooms with your Fire Blaster or hit them with your staff, then feed them to your sidekick.

Unless the GrubTubs are asleep, they will hop out of the way before you can collect them. Stun the mushrooms with your Fire Blaster, then Harvest them and feed them to Tricky. Once fed, Tricky will follow your commands.

12 SIDEKICK ASSISTANCE
◄SIDEKICK COMMANDS

You'll need Tricky's help to get across the wide lava pool. Use his Find Secret command to uncover a ground panel, then have him stay on the panel as you look for a switch that will make a platform rise from the pool.

Have Tricky dig at a dirt patch to uncover a panel on the ground. Placing pressure on the panel will open a gate that is blocking a cave. Have Tricky stay on the panel, then hit a switch in the cave. A platform will rise from the lava pool, giving you access to the other side.

14 SAVE YOUR SIDEKICK
◄HEEL COMMAND

After you enter SnowHorn Wastes, Tricky will run off ahead. Catch up to him and defeat the pack of SharpClaws attacking him. Fight off the beasts using your staff and a collection of Control Stick-triggered attack combinations. After the fight, you'll learn the Heel command.

15 PUMP UP THE POWER

At the base of a fallen tree, Tricky will discover a buried secret. After you have him dig a hole, beams of green light will pour out of an underground chamber. Drop into the hole and collect a staff energy upgrade. Your staff power meter will grow, giving you more gem-carrying capacity.

Your Controller will rumble as you approach the dirt patch near the fallen tree. Tell Tricky to dig a hole there, then drop in and collect a staff energy upgrade. The added energy reserve will allow you to use your staff more effectively.

HUNGRY, HUNGRY SNOWHORN

A mighty SnowHorn stands on the perimeter of SnowHo Wastes. It's no use trying to talk to the SnowHorn after nig falls, but if you talk to the beast in the daylight, he will tell y that he needs food. SnowHorns eat Alpine Roots.

I'm too hungry to talk to strangers.

ROOT OUT SOME FOOD
◀ALPINE ROOT

You'll find two Alpine Roots buried among the rocks and logs of SnowHorn Wastes. Both roots are under dirt patches, close to the rock wall that rings the area. Use Tricky to find both roots, then feed them to the hungry mammoth.

Alpine Roots are topped with two leaves. If you see leaves sticking out of a dirt patch on the ground, you'll know that the prize buried under the patch is SnowHorn chow.

As long as you feed Tricky, he will be able to find food for the SnowHorn. A question mark above Tricky's head will indicate that he is close to a secret. Instruct him to dig then and there.

16 ONE ROOT, A VALUABLE GIFT
◀SMALL SCARAB BAG

Once you have at least one Alpine Root, return to SnowHorn and give him the crunchy treat. The Snowl will respond by giving you a gift—the Small Scarab Bag, w gives you the ability to hold up to 50 Scarabs at a time.

By collecting Scarabs, you'll be able ..

The Small Scarab Bag t you collect from the SnowHorn can hold 50 Scarabs. When you ret the ThornTail Hollow St with the bag, you'll hav increased buying power

ANOTHER ROOT, A BIG FAVOR

...er you give a second Alpine Root to the SnowHorn, he will do
...u a favor that will get you one step closer to your goal. With a
...und-shaking stomp,
...mammoth will shut
...a nearby geyser, caus-
...a large ice block to fall
...the ground. You can
...the block for a boost
...of the area.

SnowHorns eat a lot of food. After the SnowHorn has had a second helping of
Alpine Roots, he'll stomp the ground with two heavy feet and shut off the
geyser in the center of the SnowHorn Wastes. With the geyser gone, the ice
block that it carried will fall to the ground.

BLOCK BOOST

...r of Fuel Cells rest on a ledge, out of your reach. You can use the
...ock as a step up to the ledge. Face the block, press the A Button
...lide the big cube to the edge of the ledge.

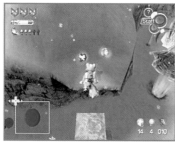

18 UP AND OUT

You can slide the block on the ice but not on the snow-packed ground.
Push the block to an area where the ice reaches the base of the wall,
then use the block for a boost up to the ledge.

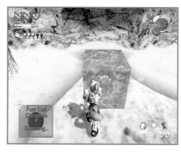

FLOE HOP

...e switch on the outside wall of the pond to make an ice floe pop
...the surface of the water. Hop from one floe to the next for access
... Fuel Cells.

19 PAY AND PASS

The SharpClaw guard who blocks the tunnel wants Scarabs.
Collect 25 Scarabs from baskets and from under rocks in the
area and hand them over to the guard. He'll step aside.

Pay the BribeClaw 25 Scarabs. He'll stand aside and let you enter. Follow
the tunnel, go with the flow of the water and make your way back to
ThornTail Hollow.

...ARTH SECRETS

...the slope from the ice floe-filled pond, you'll discover a few
... where Tricky can dig up secrets. One secret leads to a Bafom-
...Another one leads to a Fuel Cell-holding cave.

The end of the tunnel is blocked by a gate. Trigger a nearby wall switch to
make the gate drop. After you open the gate, Tricky will run off to join his
mother.

THORNTAIL HOLLOW

Your return to ThornTail Hollow will reunite Prince Tricky with the Queen EarthWalker. The queen is in poor health. She needs help in the form of six White GrubTubs. Your new task is to harvest the mushrooms from the ancient well.

It looks like she'll need a lot.

CHECKLIST

- [ ] Visit the Queen EarthWalker.
- [ ] Buy a Firefly Lantern and enter the ancient well.
- [ ] Collect the Rocket Boost upgrade.
- [ ] Heal the queen with White GrubTubs.
- [ ] Return to SnowHorn Wastes.

• **NEXT: Save the SnowHorn GateKeeper**

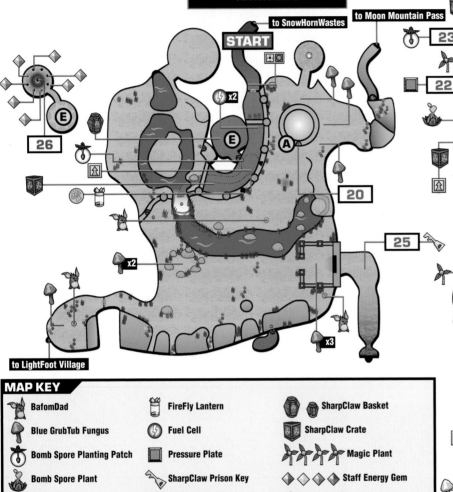

to SnowHornWastes

to Moon Mountain Pass

START

to LightFoot Village

MAP KEY

BafomDad	**FireFly Lantern**	**SharpClaw Basket**
Blue GrubTub Fungus	**Fuel Cell**	**SharpClaw Crate**
Bomb Spore Planting Patch	**Pressure Plate**	**Magic Plant**
Bomb Spore Plant	**SharpClaw Prison Key**	**Staff Energy Gem**
Token Well	**Rocket Boost Pad**	**White GrubTub Fungus**
FireFly	**Staff Rocket Boost**	

BUY SUPPLIES

◀FIREFLY LANTERN

The chamber at the bottom of the well, where White Grub-Tubs grow, is dark. Buy a FireFly Lantern in the store before you go. You can buy FireFlies, too.

20 | DIG IN AND START EXPLORING

Load up on Bomb Spores, then head for the well. You'll [...] Tricky to dig into the ancient well, but once you enter, yo[...] leave Tricky behind. Drop in and start exploring.

BLAST AND BOOST
◀STAFF ROCKET BOOST

You'll find a Bomb Spore Planting Patch in the middle of a shallow pond. Plant a spore and blast the new plant to drain the pool and reveal a hole. Drop down into the hole to receive the Rocket Boost upgrade for your staff. The new staff power will allow you to blast off from Rocket Boost Pads and reach otherwise unreachable heights.

▌DOWN YOU GO

…hornTail in the cave will step aside when he sees that you have a lantern. Use …b Spore on his former resting spot to blow open a deep hole.

MUSHROOM MOVE
◀WHITE GRUBTUBS

White GrubTubs grow down below. You can drop into the hole, but you should take the ladder to avoid a damaging fall. Grab onto the ladder and press A to slide down quickly. You'll find a White GrubTub at the bottom.

▌CUT IT DOWN TO SIZE

…e of the cave's darkest chambers, you'll discover a Planting Patch …a pillar. Plant and blast to take a chunk out of the pillar. You'll use …p of the shorter pillar as a platform.

…he base of the pillar with a Bomb Spore Plant, then climb up to the main …nd use the Rocket Boost to reach a high ledge.

22 PANEL PUZZLE

Use your Rocket Boost to reach the rock bridge above the drained pool. Grow and detonate a Bomb Spore plant on the bridge. A rock chunk will drop. Push the rock onto a ground panel to open a gate.

Blast off! You'll fly up to a natural rock bridge that reaches over the drained pool. Place a spore on the bridge and blast the plant. A piece of the bridge will drop into the pool.

Grab the bridge chunk and push it onto a ground panel. The pressure on the panel will cause the gate in the area to open, giving you access to the next chamber.

LIGHT YOUR WAY
◀FIREFLIES

Before you explore the darkest areas of the underground, you'll need fuel for your light source. You'll find three FireFlies in the immediate area. Collect them all.

CROSS AND COLLECT

Jump from a ledge to the top of the shortened pillar, then jump again to the next ledge. You'll find more GrubTubs on the other side. Once you have six mushrooms, return to the surface.

25 | CURE THE QUEEN
◀ SHARPCLAW PRISON KEY

Feed six of your White GrubTubs to the Queen EarthWalker. When she comes to, she'll ask you to talk to the GateKeeper of the SnowHorn Wastes and she'll give you a key for the SharpClaw Prison, where you'll find the dinosaur.

STOCK UP AT THE STORE
◀ CHEAT TOKEN

The buying power that y gain from having the Sm Scarab bag makes a few items in the ThornTail S a BafomDad Holder and Cheat Token—affordabl Lean over the edge of th Cheat Well in the lobby toss 20 Scarabs into th darkness.

26 | FLY UP AND DROP DOWN

Blast off from the Rocket Boost Pad near the opening of the store to reach a Bomb Spore Planting Patch on a high ledge. Blast your way into a cave, fire on four Blast Switches then drop into a hole. You'll reach another staff energy upgrade.

SNOWHORN WASTES

Your return to SnowHorn Wastes will center on the exploration of a new area, where you will take on an army of SharpClaws. Be prepared for a big battle and be on the lookout for Fuel Cells. You'll need a total of five cells to take off for the DarkIce Mines.

CHECKLIST
- [ ] Open the SharpClaw Prison Gate.
- [ ] Save the SnowHorn GateKeeper from the ice.
- [ ] Return to the Arwing and take off.

• NEXT: Fly to DarkIce Mines

MAP KEY

BafomDad		Pressure Plate	
Blue GrubTub Fungus		Scarabs	
Token Well		SharpClaw Crate	
Frost Weed		Magic Plant	
Fuel Cell		Staff Energy Gem	
Prison Gate		Rocket Boost Pad	
Fire Blast Switch			

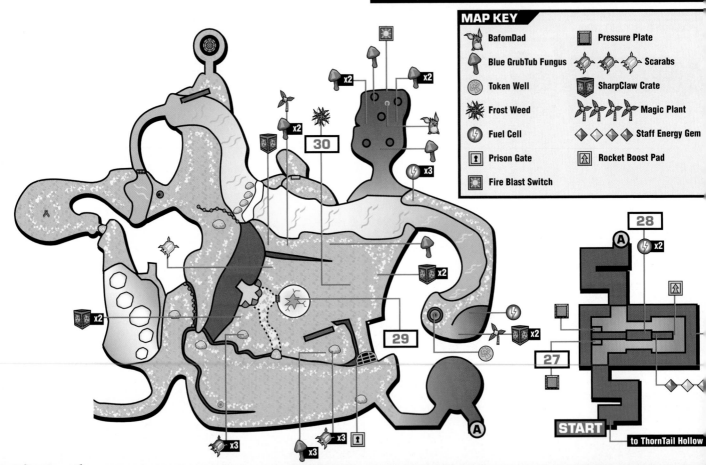

GO THE OTHER WAY

...n you reach the pressure plate in the middle of the tunnel, tell ...y to stay on the plate and climb up to an open gate. Hit a switch ...ange the flow of the water, then swim around to the other side.

...Tricky wait on a pressure plate, then climb up to a switch and hit it to change ...ow of the water in the area. You'll clear the way to SnowHorn Wastes.

28 BOOST UP FOR FUEL

You'll find a Rocket Boost Pad on a water-covered platform between the two water pipes in the ThornTail Hollow-SnowHorn Wastes tunnel. Blast off from the pad to a ledge that holds two Fuel Cells.

On your way around the water-flow puzzle area, you'll discover a new place to boost. After you land on the ledge, turn around to face the wall and hit a Fire Blast Switch. A gate will rise, giving you access to Fuel Cells.

SAVE THE SHOWHORN

...e SnowHorn Prison Key will give you access to an area near ...e river that you could not reach before. After you enter the ...ison, veer left and ...ok for SnowHorn ...teKeeper Garunda ...in a patch of ice. He'll ...k for your help. Fight ...SharpClaws, knock ...st Weeds from a tree ...arby and have Tricky ...ke them to the Gate-...eper.

...e SnowHorn GateKeeper is frozen in ice. After you talk to him about his ...dicament, SharpClaws will attack. Take them on, one at a time.

30 FIND FOOD

◄FROST WEED

The SnowHorn will be able to break out of his icy prison if he eats enough Frost Weeds. You'll find them in a tree down the hill. Hit the tree to knock them free.

Hit the tree down the hill to make Frost Weeds drop to the ground, then instruct Tricky to collect the weeds and feed them to the SnowHorn.

Fight off the SharpClaws while Tricky takes weeds to Garunda Te. When the SnowHorn has had enough, he will break free.

WITH THE FLOW

...'ll find a magic well down the river. Hop onto an ice floe and ride it ...und the bend. After you take the turn, jump onto the far shore and ...rch for the well. When you find it, toss in 20 Scarabs to get a Cheat ...en.

STOP FIRE UP THE ARWING

The SnowHorn GateKeeper has opened up the gate in the sky that will give you access to DarkIce Mines. There, you will begin your search for a missing SpellStone. Return to the Arwing with Tricky and blast off.

Go to DarkIce Mines pg. 82

Returning from DarkIce Mines with the first SpellStone, you will discover that the stone's rightful place is in the Volcano Force Point Temple in Moon Mountain Pass. After a quick stopover in ThornTail Hollow, you'll be on your way.

You got to help us!

Don't forget about the SpellStone, Fox.

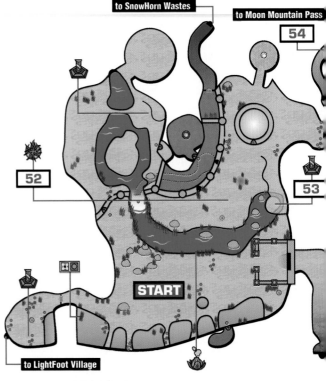

to SnowHorn Wastes
to Moon Mountain Pass
54
52
53
START
to LightFoot Village

MAP KEY

- Beacon
- Fire Weed
- Bomb Spore Plant
- Bomb Spore Planting Patch
- Staff Switch

52 WHACK THE WEEDS

◄FIRE WEEDS

The hollow's beacons are extinguished, but one of the trees near the river is on fire. Hit the tree to make Fire Weeds drop to the ground. Chase the weeds, put them out and collect them.

53 RESTORE THE LIGHT

The dinosaurs are distressed. Renegade SharpClaws have extinguished the hollow's three beacons. Collect Fire Weeds from the flaming tree and use them to light the beacons.

You'll find one of the unlit beacons on a cliff that overlooks the queen's chamber. Run up to the edge of the cliff and place a Fire Weed on the beacon. Then call Tricky and have him set fire to the beacon with his Flame Command.

BEACON HIDEAWAY

It's easy to forget that the WarpStone's garden is part of Thor[n]Hollow because it is protected by a wall. When you venture t[o] other side of the wall, you'll find an unlit beacon. Use a Fire Wee[d] Tricky's Flame Command to restore light to the remote torch.

DARKENED CAVE BEACON

After you've climbed up to the cliff in the southeast section of th[e] low, you can leap from cliff to cliff. Hit the switch on the fall w[ith] open a cave below the cliff. Enter the cave to find a beacon.

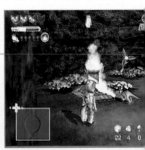

HOLLOW REWARD
◄MOON PASS KEY

Please take this. I believe it will help you on your quest.

After you find all three beacons and restore their fires, a ThornTail will reward you with a key that unlocks the SharpClaw Fortress in Moon Mountain Pass.

54 PASSAGE TO THE PASS

A sunken path near the ancient well leads to a shadowy area populated by poisonous mushrooms. Use a Bomb Spore to blast the weakened wall and enter a tunnel that leads to Moon Mountain Pass.

MOON MOUNTAIN PASS

Wide gaps and rolling barrels make Moon Mountain Pass a dangerous place. When you get to the end of the pass, you'll battle SharpClaws to gain entrance into the Volcano Force Point Temple.

CHECKLIST
- [ ] Float and jump through a windy cave.
- [ ] Survive a wave of rolling barrels as you run through the pass.
- **NEXT: Enter the Volcano Force Point Temple**

MAP KEY
- 🍄 Blue GrubTub Fungus
- ⚡ Fuel Cell
- ✳ Life-Force Door
- 🔒 Prison Gate
- 📦 SharpClaw Crate
- 🌿 Magic Plant

to Volcano Force Point Temple

x2

57

56

55

START

A

A

55 WALK INTO THE WIND TUNNEL

On your way to the Moon Mountain Pass, you'll make your way through a green-tinted tunnel, where air currents let you float up vertical passages. Jump in and watch out for wide gaps.

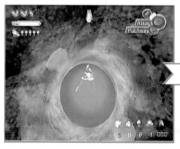

After you drop, drift to the left. When you get to the wide gap with pistonlike pillars, wait until the pillars are on their way down before you jump. Timing is critical, because the tunnel is full of potentially damaging poisonous gas.

56 BARREL BARRAGE

Donkey Kong is not the only video game villain who uses barrels to flatten advancing heroes. As you brave Moon Mountain Pass, a pair of Sharp-Claw guards will release a wave of rolling barrels. Look for rock formations to hide behind, collect a Fuel Cell as you avoid barrels and wind your way up the pass.

57 CHARGE THE GATE

When you get to the source of the barrel barrage, open the gate with the Moon Pass Key, run up to the guard's station and engage with the baddies.

One of the guards is equpped with heavy armor and a shield. Look for an opening and attack with speed and precision. After the battle, head for the temple.

VOLCANO FORCE POINT TEMPLE

As part of your effort to bring the pieces of Dinosaur Planet back together, you must return the SpellStones to where they belong. The first stone belongs in the fiery Volcano Force Point Temple.

CHECKLIST

- [ ] Enter the Volcano Force Point Temple.
- [ ] Find the Ice Blast upgrade and extinguish torches.
- [ ] Put the SpellStone in its proper place.

• NEXT: Explore Moon Mountain Pass

58 PLATFORM ZIGZAG

When you reach the long, rectangular lava pit, wait for three platforms to extend from the inner walls. Hop in a zigzag pattern from one platform to the next before they retract.

59 FIRE DOWN BELOW

A flame rises from a hole in the floor of the stone fortress. When the fire dies for a moment, drop into the hole and continue your quest on the lower floor.

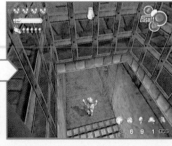

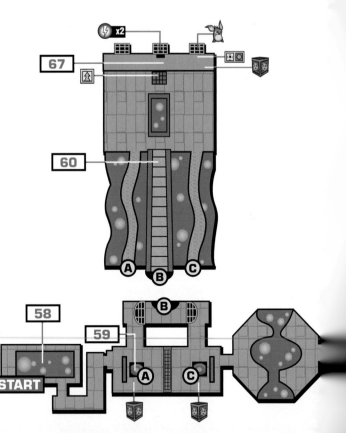

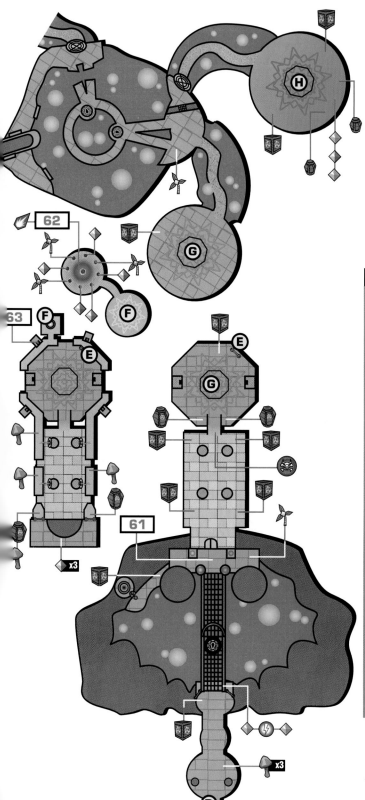

60 TEMPLE TRIALS

On your way to the entrance of the Volcano Force Point Temple, you'll climb a fire-protected conveyor belt, leap over a chasm and climb a rock wall—all in one day in the life of an adventuring fox.

61 SPELLSTONE KEY

Use the SpellStone to roll away the gate at the grand entrance, then light two orbs with magic fire and use the SpellStone again to enter the temple.

Use the SpellStone to roll away the gate, then line up a shot that goes through one of the torches and hits an orb. Wait until the color of the torch matches the color of the orb, then fire.

After you light one orb, use the same method to light the other orb. With both orbs lit, you will be able to place the SpellStone in the temple door to gain entry.

SHARPCLAW SURPRISE

A Life-Force Door blocks your way in the main hall. After you spend a few moments in the hall by yourself, four SharpClaws will materialize. Defeat them to dissolve the force field.

MAP KEY

BafomDad		SharpClaw Basket	
Blue GrubTub Fungus		SharpClaw Crate	
Ice Blast (staff upgrade)		Magic Plant	
Life-Force Door		Staff Energy Gem	
Rocket Boost Pad		Staff Switch	

◄ICE BLAST

Enlist Tricky to light two furnaces in the tall, round room. A pair of platforms will activate on the ledge above. Climb up the ladder, run along the ledge and find a green, glowing hole. Drop into the hole to earn the Ice Blast staff upgrade.

You'll find two square furnace openings in the wall. Use Tricky's Flame Command to light them. The fires will cause a pair of platforms to appear above you. Climb up the ladder and start hopping.

Take a round-trip tour of the ledge that circles the room and run through a hall-way to a glowing hole. Drop into the hole and upgrade your staff with the freezing Ice Blast power.

The Ice Blast gives you the power to extinguish torches in the room. Run along the ledge and put out each of the red fires. When you're done, an elevator will rise up from below, into the center of the room. Ride it down to a massive cavern.

Use the freezing mist of the Ice Blast to extinguish the torches that ring the room. When the last fire is out, an elevator platform will appear.

Ride the elevator down to a huge underground chamber and place the SpellStone into an indentation on a ledge to unlock a circular portal.

LIGHTS OUT

A flame blocks your way to the unlocked portal. You can walk through the flame, taking minimal damage, but you don't have to. Hit it with an Ice Blast to put it out, then move on to another elevator.

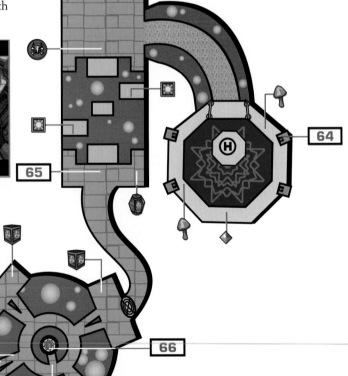

64

65

66

FOUR MORE FLAMES

[Yo]u soon reach another room, which has torches that line an upper [ledg]e. Climb a ladder to the ledge and extinguish the flames to break [the s]eal on another portal.

THE BATTLE HEATS UP

After a victory against SharpClaws that dissolves a Life-Force Door, you will face flame jets and a long lava pool. Avoid the flames and hop on floating platforms to cross the pool.

TRICKY PUZZLE

[Trick]y is not adventurous enough to take on flame jets and moving [platf]orms. When you get to the other side, turn around and look for [two]Blast switches on the [platf]orms. After you hit the [switc]hes, the platforms will [lock] into place, giving Tricky [a saf]e path across the pit. [Whe]n Tricky gets to your [side,] use him to light a fur-[nace.] The fire will break the [seal] of a nearby portal, allow-[ing y]ou to move on.

66 THE STONE'S HOME

A midtemple warp will take you to the SpellStone's chamber. As soon as you enter the room, place the stone on the pedestal in front of you. The SpellStone will float to its resting place.

Warp to a huge blue-tinted room and place the SpellStone in the pedestal before you. The SpellStone will float up to its resting place in the center of the chamber.

FREEZE FOR FUEL

On your way out of the temple, stop in the chamber that has three alcoves on a ledge. Rocket-Boost up to the ledge, grab the BafomDad and freeze the flame under the center alcove. A gate will rise, giving you access to two Fuel Cells.

KRAZOA ENCOUNTER

and collect the remaining Krazoa Spirits.

After you leave the Volcano Force Point Temple, you'll hear Krystal's cries for help and a Krazoa Spirit will appear. The spirit wants you to take a test. You'll learn more about the test as you continue your adventure.

MOON MOUNTAIN PASS

The upper area of Moon Mountain Pass is a crater-filled moonscape with mean creatures and lots of ledges. By defeating the creatures, you'll earn MoonSeeds, which you'll use to climb the cliffs.

CHECKLIST
- [ ] Earn the Ground Quake Upgrade.
- [ ] Plant MoonSeeds, climb vines and explore the upper Moon Mountain Pass.
- [ ] Collect pieces of a fallen meteor and use them to move on.
- • Take the Krazoa Test of Combat

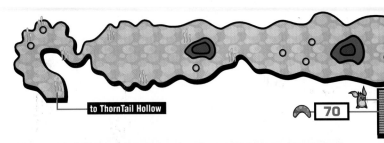

to ThornTail Hollow

68 EARTH-SHAKING DISCOVERY

◀ GROUND QUAKE

Before the Krazoa Spirit disappears, he will open the door to a tunnel that will lead you to a new staff upgrade. The Ground Quake gives you the power to shake the surrounding area and stun enemy attackers.

69 SHAKE, SPIN AND WIN

◀ MOONSEEDS

The creatures that pop from craters are tough. Shake them with your Ground Quake power to make them spin, then hit them on their backs. Every one of the creatures that you defeat will leave a MoonSeed behind.

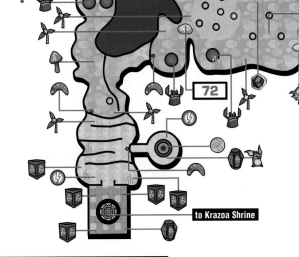

START

to Krazoa Shrine

MAP KEY

BafomDad	Token Well	Kalda Chom	SharpClaw Basket
Blue GrubTub Fungus	Fuel Barrel Generator	Meteorite Chunk	SharpClaw Crate
Bomb Spore Planting Patch	Fuel Cell	MoonSeed Planting Patch	Magic Plant
Bomb Spore Plant	Ground Quake Staff Upgrade	Scarabs	Staff Energy Gem

PLANT AND CLIMB

...onSeeds grow into vines when ...osed to extreme heat. Bury a ...d in a MoonSeed Planting Patch ...d tell Tricky to hit the seed with a ...rst of flame. The seed will break ...d produce a vine, allowing you to ...nb up to the ledge above.

...RA LIVES

...ct MoonSeeds from your battles with the crater-borne Kalda ...ns, plant the seeds and climb the vines. You'll find two life-restor-...afomDads and a Bomb Spore Plant.

The creatures in the craters can be difficult to deal with, but you will have some help. As you explore the ledges, you'll find two BafomDads. You'll also find a Bomb Spore Plant. Be sure to max out on Bomb Spores. You'll need them later.

71 ## EXPLORE THE MOONSCAPE

After you collect Bomb Spores from the Bomb Spore Plant, jump ledges and cross a bridge to a windy tunnel. You'll reach a crater creature and planting patch. Do away with the beast, then plant a spore in the patch and blast through a weak wall. You'll be on your way to the next moonscape section, where more puzzles await.

ROCK COLLECTION

...er you break through the weak wall, you'll find a passage that is ...cked by a fallen meteor. The meteor rests on one of several steam ...ts. By finding three ...aller pieces of the rock ...placing them on top of ...er steam vents, you can ...rect the steam flow and ...se the large rock to rise ...of the way. You'll find ...of the rocks out in the ...n, and Tricky will dig up ...others.

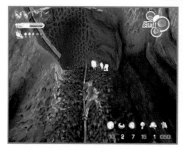 

Search for small pieces of the meteor and place them on top of steam vents. You'll have to cool one of the rocks with the Ice Blast.

Two of the smaller rocks are buried in the dirt. Use Tricky to uncover them. Pick them up and place one on each of the bottom three vents.

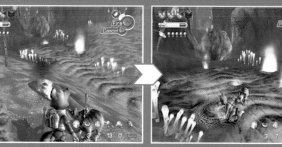 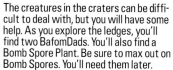

ESCAPE FROM MOON MOUNTAIN PASS

After you clear the meteor blockade, you'll climb another vine and enter a zigzag path that leads to the upper reaches of Moon Mountain Pass. At the top, you'll reach a warp that will take you to your next set of challenges.

A CELL AND A WELL

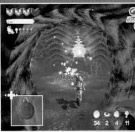

If you saved an extra MoonSeed, you'll be able to plant one last vine on your way to the warp. Climb the vine to discover a cave that holds a BafomDad, a Fuel Cell and a well.

KRAZOA TEST OF COMBAT

The Krazoa Spirits need your help. By passing the Krazoa Test of Combat, you will collect a spirit that you must take to the Krazoa Palace. The test is an obstacle course, followed by a big battle.

CHECKLIST

☐ Find the Krazoa Spirit.
☐ Take the Test of Combat.

• NEXT: Explore the lower pass

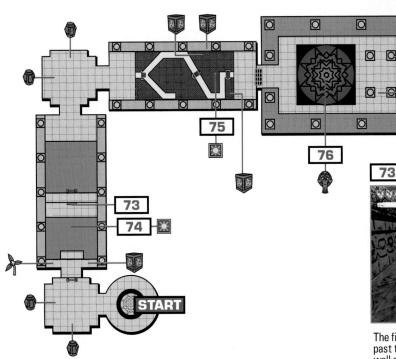

MAP KEY

⬚ Fire Blast Switch

🏺 Krazoa Spirit

🏺🏺 SharpClaw Basket

📦 SharpClaw Crate

🌱🌱🌱🌱 Magic Plant

73 WATER AND FIRE

The first obstacle is composed of a pair of whirlpools and a blocking flame. S[...] past the whirling water and use your Ice Blast to extinguish the flame. Climb[...] wall out of the pool and continue.

74 DIVE INTO THE DEEP END

When you get to the edge of the second pool, you'll see that the water level is very low—so low that you can't climb out of the other side. Turn around and hit a Fire Blast Switch near the ceiling to make the water level rise to the top of the pool.

75 TRIAL BY FIRE

A narrow, angled walkway reaches over a deep pit. As you mak[...] way over the pit, you'll encounter three fire geysers. Wait fo[...] geyser to shut off for a moment, then cross. When you reach the[...] side, turn around and hit a Fire Blast Switch to lift the next ga[...]

TAKE THE TEST OF COMBAT

e Test of Combat pits you against an
ny of SharpClaws and gives you only a
w minutes to defeat them all. As soon
the enemies begin to materialize, run
to one of them and start fighting.
me SharpClaws have shields. Hit
em immediately after they swing their
apons and don't relent.

TEST 2 - THE TEST OF COMBAT

The Krazoa Spirit will introduce you to the Test of
Combat and call a group of
powerful SharpClaws. Jump
into the fight right away and
take them out one at a time.

Your staff upgrade powers can help you in
the battle with the SharpClaw masses.
The most effective upgrade is the Ice
Blast. Freeze the enemies, then hit them
with your staff to finish them off.

OON MOUNTAIN PASS

success in the Test of Combat has earned you a Krazoa Spirit.
re you can continue your quest for the SpellStones, you must take
spirit to Krazoa Palace. And before you warp to the palace, you
t cross a new section of Moon Mountain Pass.

CHECKLIST

- [ ] Cross a chasm and break into a tunnel.
- [ ] Leave Moon Mountain Pass for ThornTail Hollow.

• NEXT: Warp to Krazoa Palace

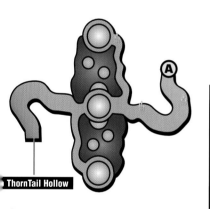

ThornTail Hollow

MAP KEY

Fuel Barrel Generator	
Kalda Chom	
SharpClaw Crate	
Magic Plant	

TRANSPORT EXPLOSIVES

 your way back to the main section of Moon
untain Pass, you'll reach a wide gap with a weak
ll on the other side. Grab a barrel and toss it to a
tural rock formation in the middle of the gap.
at over to the rock pedestal and toss the barrel at
e wall to create an opening.

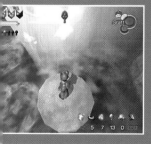
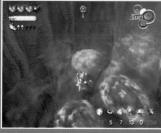

Toss the barrel into the
whirling wind so that it
floats safely to the
pedestal. Cross over to
the pedestal, grab the
barrel and throw it
across the gap to break
through the weak wall.

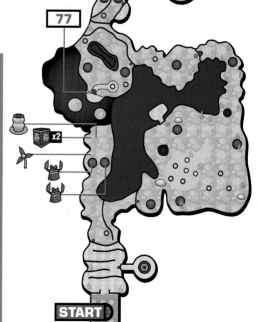

START

WIND TUNNELS IN REVERSE

When you reach the green-tinted wind tunnel section, you'll know that you're close to ThornTail Hollow. Drop into the first vertical tunnel, drift to the left ledge and wind your way to the hollow.

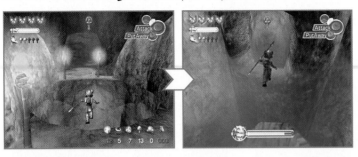

Are you ready to go to Krazoa Palace?

During your first meeting with the WarpStone, he told you that he would send you to Krazoa Palace if you had a Krazoa Spirit. Return to the WarpStone with the spirit and take him up on his offer.

KRAZOA PALACE

The Krazoa Spirit belongs in Krazoa Palace. Before you can return the spirit to its resting place, you must navigate your way through the traps and puzzles of the palace. When you reach the top, you will release the spirit and learn more about your quest.

CHECKLIST

- [ ] Survive the trials of Krazoa Palace.
- [ ] Find Krystal and return the Krazoa Spirit to its rightful place.
- • NEXT: Venture on to LightFoot Village

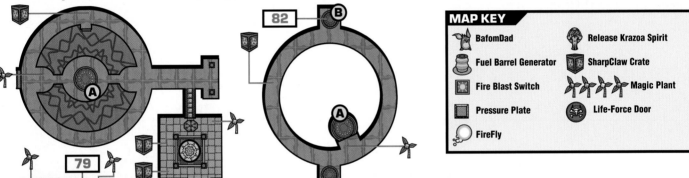

MAP KEY

🐾	BafomDad	🌿	Release Krazoa Spirit
🛢	Fuel Barrel Generator	📦	SharpClaw Crate
▦	Fire Blast Switch	🌾	Magic Plant
▢	Pressure Plate	💀	Life-Force Door
◯	FireFly		

BOX OF FLIES

Early on in your Krazoa Palac adventure, you will find seve crates containing FireFlies. Y need them for the dark secti that's coming up. Fill up on FireFlies and move on.

78 TEST OF COMBAT, PART 2

A Life-Force Door blocks the entrance to the palace. When four S Claws show up, you can clear them away quickly with an explosiv rel and your staff. After they're gone, the Life-Force Door disappear.

RUN THROUGH THE DARKNESS

The first Krazoa Palace interior section is an unlit warehouse with ramps, barriers and one weak wall. Pick up an explosive barrel from the area outside of the room, turn on the FireFly Lantern and head up the ramp to the right as soon as you enter the darkness. Navigate the ramps counterclockwise around the room and take a ramp down to the ground floor. Then break through the weak wall section.

BEAT THE MACHINE

re you can open the palace door by using the floor panel, you deal with the flame-spitting machine. Line up shots that pass ugh the color-changing torches and hit the orbs on either side of machine when the colors match. Then attack the machine itself.

RISE WITH THE WIND

a rising platform and run through a tunnel to a large, open cham- ump into the rising winds and make your way to the top floor. ore the floor and ride another wind lift to the roof.

Make your way to the open room where the wind rises. Float to the wind lift in the center of the room and let the current take you to a high wind lift on one side of the chamber. Ride the wind lift's current to the top floor, then look for another lift to the left to reach the roof.

80 WILD FIRE

Two facing flame jets block your way to a weak wall section. If you try to carry a barrel through the fire, it will blow up before you can reach the wall. Hit a Fire Blast Switch above the cracked wall section to make the flame jets slide back and forth in opposite directions, then pick up a barrel and slip past the flames.

PUT PRESSURE ON THE PLATE

After the machine is gone, fetch a barrel from the previous room, navigate past the moving flame jets and place the barrel on the pressure plate. The door will open, giving you access to the next area.

83 RELEASE THE SPIRIT

When you arrive on the palace roof, you'll see Krystal, locked in her crystal cage. Go up to where she is being held, then search the sides of the massive structure that holds Krystal's floating prison and find the frozen face of a Krazoa. You can release the spirit to its place in the palace and find out where your quest will take you next.

WARPSTONE REWARD

The WarpStone is a tough rock to crack, but you can count him as one of your friends after you return from Krazoa Palace. He'll give you a clue about where you might find the second SpellStone, and he'll hand over an item that will help you get there—the Medium Scarab Bag.

Time for you to head down to the Seaside.

Ready for you when you needed it.

LIGHTFOOT VILLAGE

Your first journey to LightFoot Village will take you through a narrow wooded area and a rock-wall maze. It's just a quick stop on your way to Cape Claw. Later, you'll explore the village proper.

CHECKLIST

- [ ] Give 60 Scarabs to the Gold Scarab.
- [ ] Navigate the maze.
- NEXT: Cross the well to Cape Claw

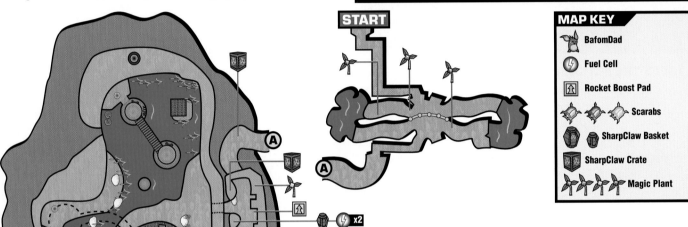

MAP KEY

- BafomDad
- Fuel Cell
- Rocket Boost Pad
- Scarabs
- SharpClaw Basket
- SharpClaw Crate
- Magic Plant

to Cape Claw

TAKE A DIP

After you emerge from the ThornT. Hollow tunnel, you'll find paths to t left and right, which both lead to w Take the path to the right, drop into water and swim to the next shore. You'll find a sign that points to LightFoot Village. When you're rea go back to ThornTail Hollow, you'll s through the other body of water.

84 PAY AND PLAY

The Gold Scarab in front of the maze gate charges admissi After you pay the statue 60 Scarabs, the gate will rise and g you access to the Cape Claw path.

EXPLORE THE LIGHTFOOT LEDGES

Across the path from the locked LightFoot Village gate, you'll find a Rocket Boost Pad that will launch you to a series of high ledges. As you run and leap from ledge to ledge, you'll discover a BafomDad and two Fuel Cells.

APE CLAW

...ould come as no surprise that Cape Claw is crawling with mem-
...of General Scales's army. A scavenger hunt and many battles
...t you on the beaches.

EP WELL, SHORT JOURNEY

On your way to Cape Claw, you'll climb down to a platform in the center of a huge well. You will find some GrubTubs, gems and Fuel Cells at the bottom of the well, but the most direct route to the next area concerns only the top floors. Drop to a circular walkway, run along the side of the well and climb a ladder up to the Cape Claw path.

CHECKLIST

- [ ] Drop into the center of the well and climb up the side.
- [ ] Get past a BribeClaw and speak to the large dinosaur.
- [ ] Collect the dinosaur's Gold Bars from the beaches.
- [ ] Free the Queen of the CloudRunners.
- [ ] Return to ThornTail Hollow.
- **NEXT: Take off for CloudRunner Fortress**

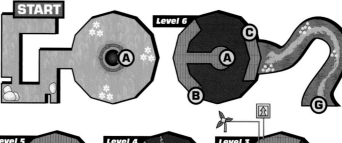
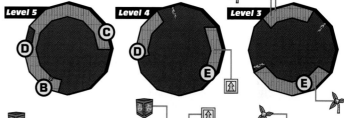
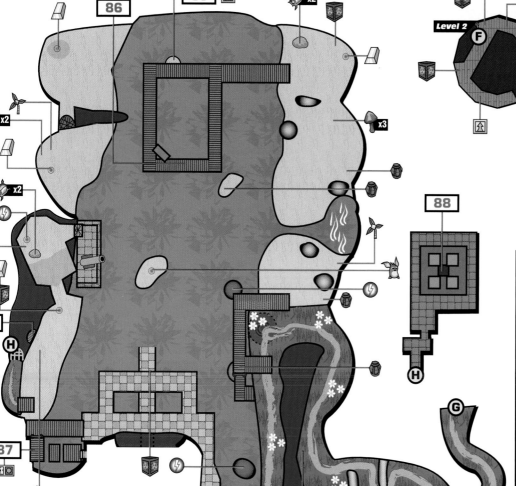

MAP KEY

- **BafomDad**
- **Blue GrubTub Fungus**
- **Fire Blast Switch**
- **Fuel Cell**
- **Rocket Boost Pad**
- **Scarabs**
- **SharpClaw Basket**
- **SharpClaw Crate**
- **Gold Bar**
- **Magic Plant**
- **Staff Switch**

HUNT AND GATHER

Serpents and GrubTubs populate the beach. You can defeat the snakes and stun the fungus with a Ground Quake attack. Gather up the mushrooms and move on.

Ground Quake creates a ground-shaking wave of energy that will defeat beach-dwelling serpents and stun sand-hopping mushrooms. Cause a quake, then run to collect Tricky's favorite food.

85 BRIBECLAW BARGAIN

A BribeClaw blocks the path to a large dinosaur who has a ques you. You can pay the BribeClaw a load of Scarabs for pier acce launch up to the walkway from a Rocket Boost Pad on a sand bar. After you reach the walkway, the BribeClaw will step aside, giving you easy beach-to-pier access.

86 DINOSAUR'S REQUEST

The occupation of Cape Claw motivated the massive dinosaur to bury his gold in the sand. He hid four Gold Bars on four different beaches in the area. Talk to him after you fight off a SharpClaw guard on the wooden walkway. He will ask you to retrieve his Gold Bars. If you manage to find all four bars and return them to the dinosaur, he will help you continue your quest.

I hid my precious gold deep below the sands.

COMB THE BEACH
◄ GOLD BAR

After your Gold Bar-rel discussion with the din take the wooden walkw and ramp to the closes beach. Tricky will alert the presence of an item buried nearby. Use your ous sidekick to dig up th first bar.

SWIM TO ANOTHER DISCOVERY

Head toward the large assembly of walkways on the cape cliffs cross the water to a beach in the shadows. You'll hear the so Queen CloudRunner coming from behind bars, but you won't be able to help her yet. Clear away a crate and tell Tricky to dig up a soft patch of sand where the crate was located. He'll unearth a Gold Bar on the spot.

...ATTLE AND A BAR

... around a large cement bulkhead to another beach and battle an ...red SharpClaw. After the fight, send Tricky on a digging quest for ...d Bar.

GIVE THE GOLD

...th all four Gold Bars in hand, return to the dinosaur. He will ...ke the ground with his mighty girth and give you access to ...other area by causing a ladder to drop.

...d the gold over to the dinosaur. He will hit the ocean floor with his feet ... shake loose a ladder on the walkway near the rock face.

...mb the ladder and hit a switch. A tunnel gate will open nearby. Climb ...wn, leap over to another walkway and head for the open path.

SAVE QUEEN CLOUDRUNNER

...ur escape from the gas chamber will open Queen CloudRun-...'s cage, too. Drop to the beach and talk to the queen for ...ormation about your next quest.

BURN YOUR WAY TO THE BEACH

Overgrown thorns block the passage to the most exclusive beach in Cape Claw. Use Tricky to burn away the bushes.

It's a good thing that there are a lot of GrubTubs on Cape Claw. You'll need the services of a well-fed sidekick. Use Tricky's Flame Command to burn away the blocking thorns. After you fight a pair of armored SharpClaws, search for the gold in shallow water.

88 FIGHT FOR FRESH AIR

On your way to the queen, you'll trigger a trap. Four big blocks will slide off poisonous gas vents. You must put the blocks back on the vents before the gas gets you.

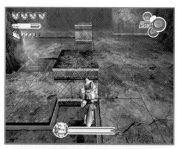 

A meter at the bottom of the screen gauges your fresh-air supply. If you are running low on fresh air as you move the blocks back onto their vents, climb up onto a rock in a corner of the room. The fresh-air meter will replenish and give you more time to move the blocks.

STOP FLY TO THE FORTRESS

Queen CloudRunner will fly back to CloudRunner Fortress. You must return to ThornTail Hollow so you can follow her. Leave the beach, run through LightFoot Village and prepare for an Arwing launch.

Go to CloudRunner Fortress pg. 94

JOURNEY TO THE OCEAN FORCE POINT TEMPLE

Your search for the second Spell-Stone's rightful place takes you back to Cape Claw, where you will find the entrance to the Ocean Force Point Temple. Before you can enter the temple, you must gather two stones and use them as temple keys.

CAPE CLAW

On your first trip to Cape Claw, you could explore the walkways of the structure that protects the Ocean Force Point Temple, but you could not enter, because you didn't have the right tools. Now that you have the SharpClaw disguise, you can go inside.

CHECKLIST

☐ Use the SharpClaw disguise to collect two Fire Gems.

☐ Place the gems in Krazoa Heads and enter the temple grounds.

• NEXT: Explore Ocean Force Point Temple

MAP KEY

- **BafomDad**
- **Blue GrubTub**
- **Fire Blast Switch**
- **Fire Gem**
- **Fuel Cell**
- **SharpClaw Crate**
- **SharpClaw Disguise Pad**
- **Pressure Plate**
- **Magic Plant**
- **Staff Switch**

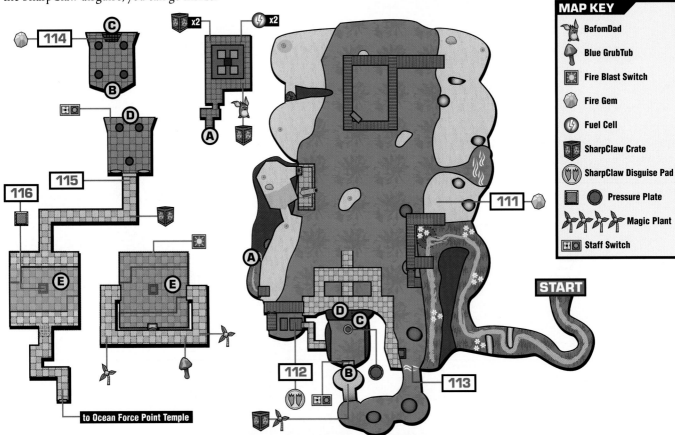

to Ocean Force Point Temple

---

111 LIBERATE A LIGHTFOOT

When you reach the beach, you'll find two SharpClaws bullying a LightFoot. Your heroic nature compels you to fight off the SharpClaws and save the helpless dinosaur.

HOT POTATO

◄ FIRE GEM

SharpClaws interrupt conversation with the LightFoot by lobbing ca balls in your direction. LightFoot "found" a Fi belonging to the SharpClaws. He'll pas hot item to you and ma escape from the canno

2 WORK AROUND THE WALL

journey takes you to the cement and wood walkways on the h wall. Climb up the ladder and leap over to a locked door. You can he SharpClaw disguise to open the door.

Run up the cement ramps to the wooden walkway and climb up the ladder that the large dinosaur dropped on your last visit to the cape. Follow the walkway to a door and use the SharpClaw disguise to enter an ancient structure.

CH THE CURRENT

n into the cave and follow the water flow around several large rock ations. You'll reach an edge and an opening to another area. Drift to the edge and drop into the opening.

FIRE IN THE HOLE

mb the walkways on the exterior wall an open entrance. You'll find two Kra- a Heads inside a large chamber. Place e Fire Gems into the statues, then use illar on the other side of the room to e Tricky a boost to the ceiling. Tricky n shed light on the mystery of the ked door from there.

After you place the Fire Gems into the Krazoa Heads, you might expect the door to open. It won't. Look around the room—you'll find a tall pillar and a hole that is blocked by thorns. If only you could get Tricky up there.

Hit a switch to make the pillar drop to floor level. Tell Tricky to stay on the pillar, then hit the switch again to have your sidekick rise to the blocked opening. Command Tricky to burn the vines and let light into the room. The light will open the large door.

113 CAVE QUEST

The water in the first temple room is deep. The only island that you can reach is a pressure plate. After you apply pressure to the plate, another island will surface. Have Tricky stay on the first island, then swim to the second island and hop to a ledge. You'll find a switch that will close off a waterfall and give you access to a cave entrance on the exterior wall.

114 FIGHT FIRE WITH ICE

A flame blocks a Krazoa Head that holds a second Fire Gem. Extinguish the flame with your Ice Blast and take the stone. The water level will rise, giving you access to the exit.

After you reach a blocking gate on the other side of a pool, turn around and shoot at a high Fire Blast Switch. The water level will rise, giving you access a new tunnel. Use Tricky to burn away thorns in the passage, then push a blo into the water and hit the Fire Blast Switch to lower the water level. Next push the block onto a gate-lifting pressure plate.

OCEAN FORCE POINT TEMPLE

Water levels and current play big parts in the puzzles of the Ocean Force Point Temple. By solving the puzzles, you will find a place to put the second SpellStone.

CHECKLIST

- [ ] **Explore the temple passages.**
- [ ] **Use Warp Pads to access the central chamber.**
- [ ] **Put the SpellStone in its proper place.**

• **NEXT:** Discover LightFoot Village

CLIMB AND CONNECT

Climb two long ladders to the top of the Ocean Force Point Temple entry cave place the SpellStone in an indentation to open the temple path.

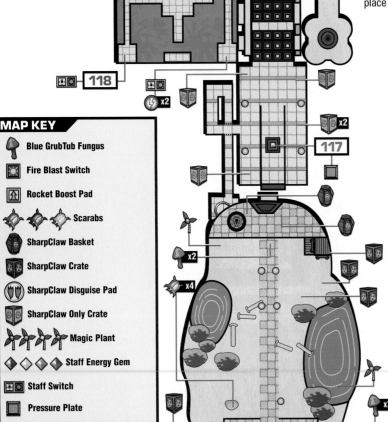

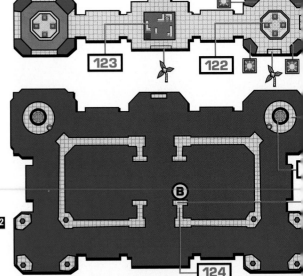

MAP KEY

- 🍄 Blue GrubTub Fungus
- Fire Blast Switch
- Rocket Boost Pad
- Scarabs
- SharpClaw Basket
- SharpClaw Crate
- SharpClaw Disguise Pad
- SharpClaw Only Crate
- Magic Plant
- ◆◇◈◇ Staff Energy Gem
- Staff Switch
- Pressure Plate

119
120
118
117
123
122
124
START

7 TILE TROUBLE

he floor of a large chamber in the
mple depths is covered with elec-
c panels. Tell Tricky to stay on a
essure plate and trigger a map of
e panels. The map will show you
e panel that you can touch first on
ch row.

FLAME ON

ll discover a network of narrow walkways over the water. When
reach the place where the walk splits into three paths, explore the
assage to find a switch that lights a fire.

Swim over to a low ledge near the raised
walkways and leap to a place where the
walkway splits into three passages.
Make your way up the left path to reach
a switch that lights the colored flame.

FIRE AND WARP

n you reach a Warp Pad, you'll see that it is not active. Line up a
through the color-changing flame to an orb. Fire when the color
e flame matches the color of the orb to activate the pad.

WATER LEVEL WAVERING

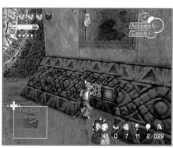

119 CUT OFF THE FLOW

After you light the fire, return to the central platform and take the
right path and middle path up to two other switches. Hit the switches
to cut off the flow of water in
the chamber, which will give
you access to a tunnel. Swim
through the tunnel and
climb a wall up to the area
with the burning flames.

BREAK AND BOOST

Cross over to the box across the water and break it to reveal a Rocket
Boost Pad. Blast off to a high ledge and grab a pair of Fuel Cells.

Hit a switch to lower the water level in
the flooded room, then hit another
switch to open the portal. Use your
SharpClaw disguise on a pad to gain
access to a block, move the block to the
ledge below the first switch, then throw
the switch to make the water level rise
again. That will give you access to the
next room.

122 DOUSE THE SPINNING TORCHES

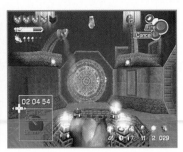

You'll discover a round hole in the wall the massive chamber that houses fou Krazoa Spirit statues and four torche on a turntable. Tell Tricky to breathe flames into the hole. The torches will light up, the turntable will begin to sp and the statue heads will fill with wa Fire-Blast the switches below the st ues to make the Krazoas lean forwar and douse the fires. Once the fires are out, a new door will open.

123 SHOOT AND SCOOT

The large block in the pit will move if you hit the round targets on its sides. Aim your shots so that the block slides into the alcove on the far corner. A successful slide will shut off the electric shockers on the ledges.

By Fire-Blasting the targets on the s of the block, you can make the block slide as far as it can go in one directi Starting from the side of the room opposite to where you entered, blas the block six times while walking around the pit in a counterclockwise pattern. After the block slides into i place, it will activate a Rocket Boos Pad in the first room.

124 NAVIGATE THE LEDGES

Return to the first room that you explored in the area and use the Rocket Boost Pad to launch up to a ledge. You'll reach a network of tunnels that connects the ledges in the area rooms. Run through the tunnels and search for a Warp Pad.

125 BRIDGE THE GAP

The Warp Pad is isolated from the ledges. As you look at the pad, y see a color-changing flame and an orb in the distance. Line up a c matching shot to make a bridge appear.

SPELLSTONE SLIDE

When you reach the SpellStone room, you'll know exactly what to d Place the stone in the pedestal before you and watch as the SpellStone slides to its resting plac

LIGHTFOOT VILLAGE

The LightFoot that you met in Cape Claw was not a bad apple in a good bunch. All of the LightFoots are a little rotten. When you emerge from the maze, a group of LightFoots will take you prisoner on the premise that you stole their Fire Gem. You must set them straight.

Hey there little fella.

Whoa... what happened? Untie me right now!

CHECKLIST

- [ ] Escape from the bonds of the LightFoots.
- [ ] Find and replace three plugs.
- [ ] Pass the two tests of the LightFoots.
- [ ] Solve a puzzle in the LightFoot shrine.
- [ ] Rescue LightFoot children.

• NEXT: Take the Krazoa Test of Fear

MAP KEY

- Blue GrubTub Fungus
- Fuel Cell
- LightFoot Totem Pole
- Rocket Boost Pad
- Wooden Block Carvings
- Scarabs
- SharpClaw Basket
- SharpClaw Crate
- Magic Plant

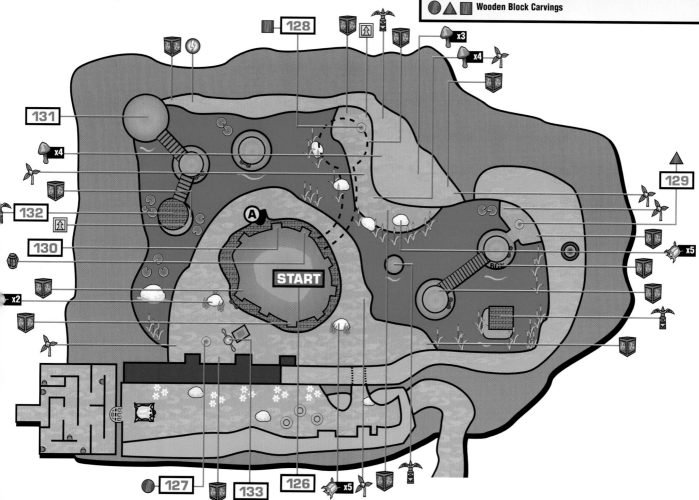

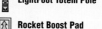

TORCH THE TRIBE

You can fight the attacking Light-foots with help from a CloudRun-r. A target marker will slide back d forth on a bar at the top of the reen. Press A when the marker s the shaded section of the bar to ke the CloudRunner swoop wn and spit fire.

127 BIG DIG DISCOVERY
◄ROUND CARVING

Three of the pedestals on the huge LightFoot Village mound are missing carved blocks. Turn around and head for the closest wall, then search the area near the pit and have Tricky dig up the Round Wooden Block Carving.

128 BURN, DIG, FIND
◄SQUARE CARVING

After you cross the narrowest section of water, you'll see a thorny blockade on a rock wall. Tell Tricky to burn the thorns to reveal a small circular area. If you have Tricky dig there, you will uncover the Square Wooden Block Carving.

129 REMOTE FIND
◄TRIANGLE CARVING

In the northeast section of the swamp, you'll find a small section of land that serves as a landing for one of the stilted huts. Have Tricky dig up the soft dirt circle on the island to reveal the last of the three block carvings.

HOP, BOOST AND CLIMB

Head for the mound in the western section of the village that has a totem pole on top. You can make your way to the base of the mound by hopping on newly formed platforms. Uncover a Rocket Boost Pad and blast off to the top of the mound. Cross the bridge to an empty hut, then climb down a ladder. You'll find another bridge that will lead you to the head of the tribe.

130 BLOCK PARTY

Return to the mound with all three blocks in hand and place the right pegs in the right holes. Each wooden block carving makes a different set of platforms rise to the surface of the water. The platforms will allow you to hop over to several otherwise unreachable LightFoot Village locations.

131 LEADER OF THE LIGHTFOOTS

The head of the LightFoot Tribe wants to test you before he helps you. He'll give you a choice between two tests, but he won't help you until you have passed both.

2 THE OLD RUNAROUND

The Tracking Test challenges you to find and trigger four totem poles in just a few minutes. The test will take you to all parts of the village. Chart a path, then run to your goals.

Immediately after you leave the leader's hut, climb up to the top of the stilted hut and cross over to the totem on the mound.

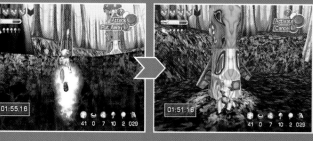

You'll find a Rocket Boost Pad in the area where you found the Square Wooden Block Carving. Blast off the pad to a totem pole.

One of the most prominent totems in the village is on the eastern side of the swamp. You can reach the goal by hopping from one platform to the next.

A totem sits on a tall brick tower in the southeast section of the swamp. You can avoid swimming against the current by swimming under the stilted huts. When you get to the base, climb the vine-covered side to the totem.

3 TWITCH TEST

The Test of Strength pits you against village strongman MuscleFoot. You must push him into the hole by way of a lever mechanism before he puts you into the hole. You'll accomplish the task by pressing the A Button repeatedly. A fast, steady rhythm is your key to success.

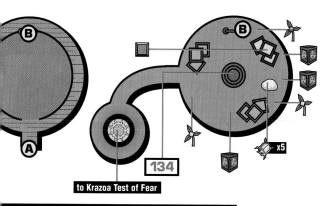

to Krazoa Test of Fear

KEY

Pressure Plate   SharpClaw Crate

Scarabs   Magic Plant

134 COMPLETE THE PICTURE

After you complete both tests, the leader of the tribe will open up a special inner sanctum. Enter the chamber, climb down a ladder and climb up to a pressure plate.

When you're on the pressure plate, individual segments of the totem in the center of the room will spin. Each segment has a piece of a serpent picture on one side. When the segment pictures line up with the picture on the totem base, fire at the segments to stop them from spinning. After the picture is compete, you will have access to a Krazoa Temple warp.

TROUBLED TRIPLETS

After you take the tests, you will earn the trust of the LightFoot tribe. If you visit the huts that were empty before you took the tests, you will find members of the tribe who will ask you to find three groups of three children each.

My babies like to climb trees.

135 SHAKE THE TREES

You'll find one of group of three missing children in trees outside of the village wall. Hit the trunks to shake the children loose.

SECRET GATE

Once you leave the village proper, the gate will close. Exit the tree-lined area and return to watch a member of the tribe unlock the gate. The key is to hit trees in a certain order.

Three trees in a row are painted with bull's-eyes. Hit the targeted tree closest to the gate with your staff, then hit the far tree and, lastly, the middle tree. The gate will open to give you you village access.

136 →

to ThornTail Hollow

135

to Cape Claw

138

137

A

to ThornTail Hollow
to Cape Claw

MAP KEY

🦇	BafomDad	🔲	Rocket Boost Pad
⊙	Token Well	🧺	SharpClaw Basket
○	FireFly	📦	SharpClaw Crate
⚡	Fuel Cell	🌿🌿🌿	Magic Plant

136 FOREST FIND

One of the LightFoot parents will tell you that her children like to play in the w
Boost up to the wooded section to find the wandering youths and shoo them
the ledge.

137 UNDERGROUND DISCOVERY

After a member of the tribe gives you a clue about the children playing underg
go to the Krazoa Shrine. You'll find LightFoot triplets on the upper level. Shoo
out the door.

8 ROCKET UP TO THE OUTER EDGE

By saving all three groups of LightFoot children, you will have access to new items: For the first group of three, you'll gain access to two Fuel Cells; the second group will make three SharpClaw Crates appear; and the third set will produce a new Rocket Boost Pad near the edge of the village. Use the pad to fly up to a ridge, and find a Fuel Cell and a BafomDad.

WELL FOUND

You'll find a Token Well on the upper ridge. You'll be able to use the token that you buy from the well to get a fortune from the well in the WarpStone's Game Well Maze.

RAZOA TEST OF FEAR

quest to collect another Krazoa Spirit starts in a series of booby-
ped chambers. After you survive flames, spikes and rolling barrels,
will help Fox face his greatest fear. If you endure the test without
hing, the spirit will possess Fox.

CHECKLIST
☐ Survive the trap-packed obstacle course.

☐ Pass the Test of Fear.

NEXT: Warp to Krazoa Palace

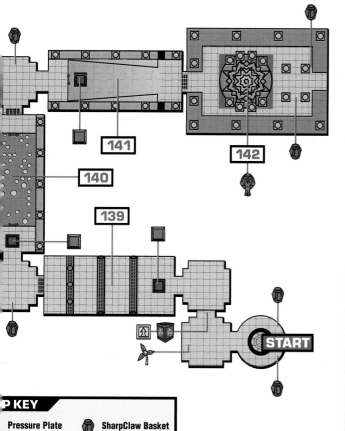

MAP KEY

Pressure Plate	SharpClaw Basket
Krazoa Spirit	SharpClaw Crate
Rocket Boost Pad	Magic Plant

139 FIRE FLIGHT

After you rocket up to the obstacle course, you will find yourself in a long chamber with a pressure plate on one end and a gate on the other end. Stand on the plate to open the gate, then run through the chamber, past several flame jets, before the gate closes.

140 SWIMMING SURVIVAL TEST

The next long chamber features a spike-filled pool. When you stand on the pressure plate, the gate will open and the pool will begin to drain. The lower the water level is, the harder it is to navigate past the spikes. Dive in quickly and avoid the middle.

141 ROLLING THUNDER

Barrels roll down a long ramp and crash when they hit the wall. Stand on a pressure plate to open the gate at the top of the ramp, then start running. Focus on one barrel at a time and zigzag out of the way. You can also roll under barrels while they're in the air.

142 FEAR FACTOR

The Test of Fear is an unsettling collection of illusions. As raptors run and leap toward Fox and a shadowy image of General Scales make a startling appearance, a re line will sway back and forth in a meter at the top of the screen. Yo must keep the line in the meter's shaded area as you face your fear by pressing Left and Right on the Control Stick.

KRAZOA PALACE

With the Krazoa Spirit surging through Fox, you must warp to the Krazoa Palace and return the spirit to its rightful place. Return to ThornTail Hollow and use the WarpStone to travel to the palace.

CHECKLIST

☐ Warp to Krazoa Palace.
☐ Return the Krazoa Spirit to its rightful place.

NEXT: Return to the ThornTail Hollow

FLY TO THE MIDDLE

Make your way to the large, open chamber and take a wind lift flight to the cha ber's second floor. Fight off SharpClaws and move on.

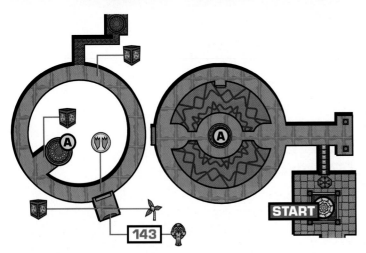

143 RELEASE THE KRAZOA SPIRIT

While exploring the second floor you will find a locked door and a SharpClaw disguise pad. Use you SharpClaw disguise to open the door. You'll find a warp to the Krazoa Spirit's resting place on t other side.

MAP KEY

🌳 Release Krazoa Spirit   〰 SharpClaw Disguise Pad

📦 SharpClaw Crate   🌱🌱🌱🌱 Staff Energy Gem Tree

HORNTAIL HOLLOW

...ore you can fly to the next SpellStone location, you must do a favor ...desperate ThornTail and earn an upgrade. The upgrade will allow ...to open the gate in the sky to the Walled City.

CHECKLIST
- [ ] Save the ThornTail eggs and collect the Portal Move.
- [ ] Open the portal door in the queen's chamber.

NEXT: Fly to Walled City

4 EGG MANIA

...xplore the WarpStone's garden to find a ThornTail mother ...ho fears for the safety of her eggs. The eggs are in the center of ...cave chamber where thieving ...reatures can enter from the ...des. A clock will begin to tick ...wn. If you can fight off the ...ieves, you will earn a staff ...grade. Use Ground Quake ...take on several thieves at ...ce.

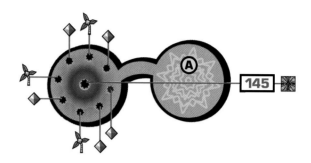
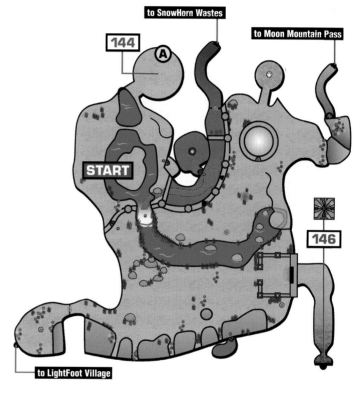

5 DROP DOWN FOR AN UPGRADE

◄ PORTAL MOVE

After you save the ThornTail eggs, the thankful mother will open up an underground cave for you. Drop into the cave to upgrade your staff. The upgrade will allow you to open special portals that are scattered throughout Dinosaur Planet.

to SnowHorn Wastes
144 Ⓐ
to Moon Mountain Pass
START
146
to LightFoot Village
145 Ⓐ

6 THE KING'S SECRET

Son, your father has been taken prisoner...

Once you have the Portal Move staff upgrade, talk to the Queen Earthwalker. She will fill you in on the King's role as a GateKeeper. Since the king is held captive in the Walled City, he can't open the Walled City space gate for you. Use your staff to open the portal behind the queen. That will open the gate.

MAP KEY

▨ Portal Move		⚘⚘⚘ Magic Plant	
▨ Portal Door		◆◇◇◇ Staff Power Gem	

STOP FLY TO THE KING

You have two reasons to fly to the Walled City—save the King Earthwalker and collect another SpellStone. The flight will be challenging and the fight in the city will be rough. Prepare yourself for a hard road ahead.

Go to Walled City pg. 104

RETURN TO MOON MOUNTAIN

The third SpellStone belongs in the Volcano Force Point Temple. After you come back from your first adventure in the Walled City, make your way through Moon Mountain Pass to the temple. Be sure to collect a MoonSeed along the way.

VOLCANO FORCE POINT TEMPLE

You'll run through a lot of familiar territory in Volcano Force Point Temple. Since you've already unlocked the doors, your journey through the opening temple sections should be quick.

CHECKLIST

☐ Enter Volcano Force Point Temple with the third SpellStone.

☐ Solve a series of new puzzles and put the stone into its place.

NEXT: Save ThornTails in ThornTail Hollow

TRIALS BY FIRE

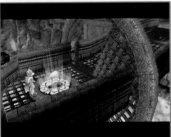

The familiar paths in the Volcano Force Point Temple are just as dangerous as they were on your first visit. Work out the timing of the platforms over lava and the flame-spewing jets, and try to make your way through the passages unharmed. You can collect two Fuel Cells along the way by opening a gate with your SharpClaw disguise.

OFF-ROAD ITEMS

If you've got your PDA set to the Fuel Cell Compass, you'll discover that there are cells off the main path, near the main gate of the temple. You'll need a MoonSeed to get to the cells and other items.

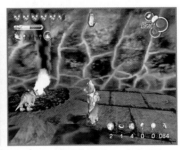

Travel west from the main gate, climb down a cliff face and plant a MoonSeed. After Tricky adds his fire to the equation, a vine will sprout. Climb the vine to two Fuel Cells, a BafomDad and a well.

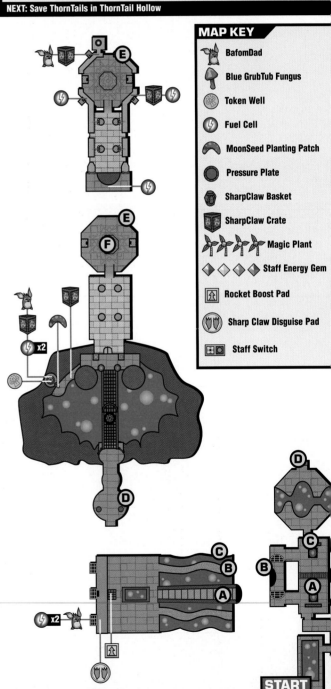

MAP KEY

🐰	BafomDad
🍄	Blue GrubTub Fungus
⊚	Token Well
⚡	Fuel Cell
⌒	MoonSeed Planting Patch
◯	Pressure Plate
🧺	SharpClaw Basket
📦	SharpClaw Crate
🌿	Magic Plant
◆◇◇◆	Staff Energy Gem
⬆	Rocket Boost Pad
👣	Sharp Claw Disguise Pad
▣	Staff Switch

START

EP CHEAT

he cave near the main gate that holds Fuel Cells and a Bafom-
ad also features a Cheat Well.

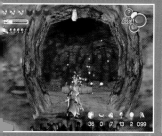 

156 OLD TEMPLE, NEW PATH

Collect two Fuel Cells on a high ledge, then take the elevator down to
the depths of the temple. You'll find a place to put the new SpellStone,
close to an indentation where you put the first SpellStone. Place the
SpellStone to open an unexplored path.

7 LAVA AND LEDGES

new passage is on the other side of a
e lava moat. You can cross the lava by
ping on floating platforms. Some of
platforms have flaming vents. Before
hop onto them, be sure to extinguish
flames with an Ice Blast. If you climb
ledges in the area, you'll find gems and
bTubs.

Drop down to the level
of the lava and hop
from one platform to
the next. Climb the
ledges and collect all of
the gems and mush-
rooms you can find.

You'll have a good view
of the room from the
top of the ledges. If you
want to take the quick
way down, you can
jump from a ledge to
the ringed walkway.

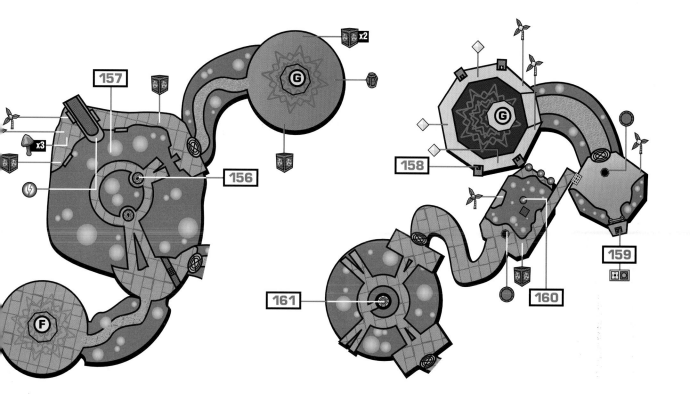

158 EXTINGUISHING ORDER

After you ride an elevator up to a new section of the temple, you'll find a ladder that leads to a high ledge. You must extinguish all of the torches on the ledge to unlock the next door. The flames will reignite after you freeze them unless you put them out in the right order: blue, green, red, then yellow. When the final flame flickers out, locking braces will disappear from the door.

Use Ice Blast to extinguish the blue torch, then the green, red and yellow torches, in that order.

160 BLASTED ORBS

You'll find three orbs on the wall of the room with a fiery platform and a pressure plate. Have Tricky stay on the plate to make the platform move and fire on the orbs through a color-changing torch.

Line up orb shots through the fire and shoot when the fire matches the color of the orbs. A color-matching shot will make the target orb glow. After you make all three orbs glow, you'll earn passage to the next room.

159 PRESSURE PLAY

Two SharpClaws will surprise you in the room with the pressure p and the out-of-reach ladder. Put the pressure on the guards, then Tricky to stay on the plate. The ladder will lower.

After you fight off the SharpClaws, instruct your sidekick to stay on the press plate. Climb the ladder that drops, then extinguish the flame at the top to revea switch. The switch will open a gate on the lower floor.

161 THE SPELLSTONE STAYS

After you open the last door, you'll warp to the resting place the Volcano Force Point Temple SpellStones. Put the templ second stone in its place, then leave for ThornTail Hollow.

Jump on the Warp Pad an return to the blue-tinted SpellStone room. After y put the SpellStone in its place, you'll find yourself the temple's main gate. From there, your adventures will take you back the hollow.

THORNTAIL HOLLOW

You'll reach ThornTail Hollow just in time to save the hollow's helpless dinosaurs. Winged creatures will emerge from the ancient well and attack the ThornTails. You must pluck them out of the air.

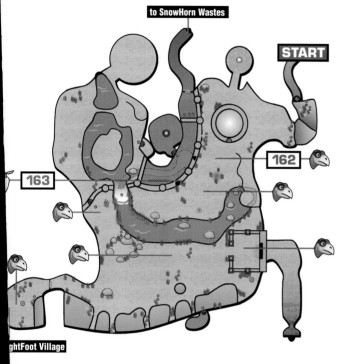

to SnowHorn Wastes

START

162

163

LightFoot Village

MAP KEY

Gold Artifact

ThornTail

CHECKLIST

☐ Save the ThornTails from an air attack to earn the Large Scarab Bag.

☐ Accumulate Scarabs, then purchase the SnowHorn Artifact.

NEXT: Venture to Snowthorn Wastes

162 BATTLE THE BATS

Winged beasts have descended upon the hollow and are swarming around six of the area's dinosaurs. Run up to the ThornTails, lift your Fire Blaster to the sky and take out the bats as they circle the big beasts. Time is tight. You must free all of the ThornTails before the bats cause too much damage.

You'll find three bats circling around each ThornTail. Get close and hit them with Fire Blaster shots.

ik, 'lo wek kxat veh oei...

One of the ThornTails is in the tunnel to LightFoot Village. After you save all six of the dinosaurs, you'll earn the Large Scarab Bag.

163 BIG BUY

◀SNOWHORN ARTIFACT

The most expensive item in the ThornTail Store is the very thing that one of the SnowHorns has been looking for. Collect a lot of Scarabs, then purchase the SnowHorn Artifact.

OK, I'll sell it to you.   146

DELIVER THE ARTIFACT

Once you have the SnowHorn Artifact, you will have what you need for a productive visit to the SnowHorn Wastes. Climb the ladder, enter the tunnel and continue your journey.

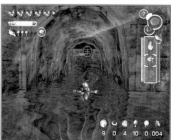

SNOWHORN WASTES

Your reward for returning the SnowHorn Artifact to its owner will be a timed tour around SnowHorn Wastes, followed by a warp trip to the next Krazoa test.

CHECKLIST
☐ Give the ShowHorn Artifact to the mammoth on the pond.
☐ Blow the Dinosaur Summon Horn on a series of pads before time expires.

NEXT: Warp to the Krazoa Shrine

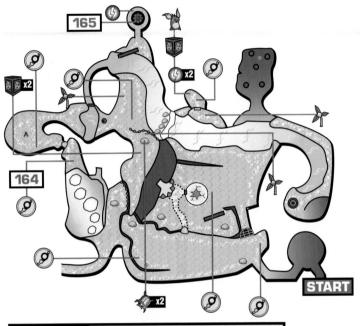

MAP KEY

BafomDad		Scarabs	
Dinosaur Horn Pad		SharpClaw Crate	
Fuel Cell		Magic Plants	

164 BRING BACK THE ARTIFACT

Shabunga claims to have "found" the SnowHorn Artifact in SnowHorn Wastes. When you return to the wastes with the item, you'll find its rightful owner.

Follow the path up to the area above the SharpClaw prison and hop across the pond to the area's lone SnowHorn. After you give the item to the SnowHorn, he will start a timer and challenge you to find a series of Dinosaur Horn Pads before the time expires.

MELT THE WALL

A Dinosaur Summon Pad will rise from the snow in an area behind the gray SnowHorn. Tell Tricky to apply heat to an ice wall that blocks your way, then run to the pad and play the horn.

Once you play the horn on the pad that emerges near the SnowHorn, another one will appear in an area behind him. Walk around the mammoth, tell Tricky to melt a barrier and look for the pad on the other side.

TRAVEL TO THE TUNNEL

After you play the horn near the river, take the most direct route to the tunnel entrance. Along the way, you will find two more Dinosaur Horn Pads. Play the horn on each pad.

CREATE A BRIDGE

Follow a trail down to the river and aim your Fire Blaster at the cr-ture in the tree on the other side of the water. The tree will fall over water, giving you quick access to a pad near the shore.

Hit the creature in the tree with a Fire Blaster shot to make the tree fall over t river. Use the fallen tree as a bridge across the water and look for a Dinosaur H Pad on the other side.

TO THE GATEKEEPER

...er the SharpClaw Prison and run to Garunda Te. You'll find a pad ...r the GateKeeper. Play the horn there, then head for the water.

Run to the GateKeeper and play the horn on another pad, then run to the water and knock over another tree.

CROSS AND CLIMB

After you knock down a tree to make a new bridge across the water, run to the other side and climb the wall. You'll find the final Dinosaur Horn Pad on a ledge.

165 WARP TO THE SHRINE

After you play the horn on the last Dinosaur Horn Pad, a cave near the water will open. Talk to the gray SnowHorn near the cave, then enter the cave and warp to the next Krazoa test.

...RAZOA TEST OF STRENGTH

...hallenging obstacle course leads to another Krazoa Spirit test. ...r you pass the test, you will have a new Krazoa Spirit to release in ...Krazoa Palace.

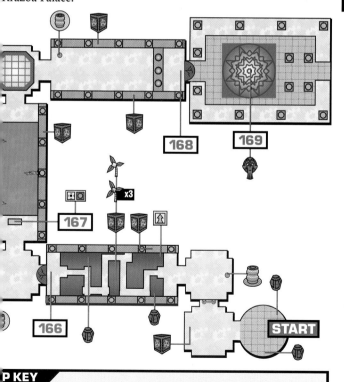

P KEY

- Fuel Barrel Generator
- Fuel Barrel Pad
- Krazoa Spirit
- Rocket Boost Pad
- SharpClaw Basket
- SharpClaw Crate
- Magic Plant
- Staff Switch

CHECKLIST

- [ ] Run through an obstacle course to the Krazoa Spirit.
- [ ] Take the Krazoa Test of Strength.

NEXT: Warp to Krazoa Palace

166 SLIP, SLIDE AND EXPLODE

You'll find a weak wall at the end of a slippery zigzag path over a pit. Fire Blast the flying creatures, then pick up a Fuel Barrel and navigate the path.

When you get to the end of the path, toss the barrel at the weak wall to open a passage to your next challenge.

167 FLIGHT OF THE FUEL BARREL

A barrel-carrying robot floats in the air over a pool. Retrieve a barrel from the previous chamber, put it on a pad and let the robot carry it away. As the robot flies, a switch to redirect the flames in the room to make sure the robot doesn't f through fire.

168 TOSS AND CARRY

After you get the barrel across the pool, throw it to the other side of a wind tunnel, then face off with a SharpClaw guard.

Fight the guard, then pick up the barrel and carry it to the other end of the long chamber. When you reach the brick obstacle, wait for the fire geyser in the center to stop for a moment and toss the barrel over the barrier to break through the wall.

169 SHOW YOUR MUSCLE

The Krazoa Spirit will pit you against a SharpClaw in a te that is very similar to the LightFoot Village Test of Strengt. Press the A Button quickly and repeatedly to push a stor turntable. When you rotate it 180 degrees, you'll pass the tes

KRAZOA PALACE

Possessed by the Krazoa Spirit, you will take a short journey to the palace and release the spirit to its place. The release point is on the other side of a Portal Door. Float up one floor and look for the door.

CHECKLIST

- [ ] Warp to Krazoa Palace.
- [ ] Return the Krazoa Spirit.

NEXT: Rturn to ThornTail Hollow

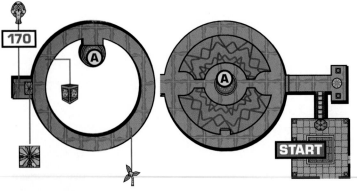

170 RELEASE THE KRAZOA SPIRIT

Use the wind lift in the large, open chamber to float up to t lowest ledge. Run around the ledge, collect a gem from a tre fight a SharpClaw, then open a Portal Door. You'll find a pla to release the spirit on the other side.

MAP KEY

- Portal Door
- SharpClaw Crate
- Release Krazoa Spirit
- Magic Plant

HORNTAIL HOLLOW

short visit to the Krazoa Palace will be followed by a short return ornTail Hollow. You'll seek out the GateKeeper then fly to on Rock.

CHECKLIST

- [ ] Find the ThornTail GateKeeper and have him open the gate.
- [ ] Prepare for an Arwing flight.

NEXT: Fly to Dragon Rock

THORNTAIL GATEKEEPER

WarpStone will tell to talk to the rnTail who does say very much. 'll find the Thorn- near the ancient . He will have ething to say—for ange.

He who has no voice has plenty to say.

He imprisoned three of my closest friends on Dragon Rock...

and speak to the ThornTail GateKeeper. He will tell you his story then the way to Dragon Rock.

172 IMPROVE YOUR SIGHT
◀HI-DEF DISPLAY DEVICE

028

If you haven't purchased the Hi-Def Display Device from the ThornTail Hollow Store yet, you should pick it up before you leave for Dragon Rock. Good long-distance vision will come in handy over the course of your adventure there.

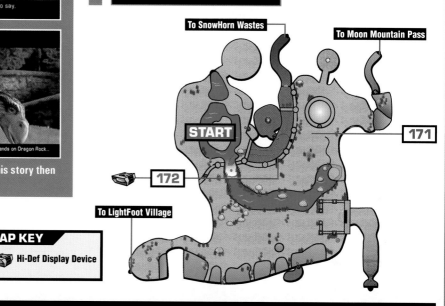

To SnowHorn Wastes

To Moon Mountain Pass

START

171

172

To LightFoot Village

MAP KEY
Hi-Def Display Device

FIND FUEL

first trip to each of Dinosaur Planet's moons requires a ain number of Fuel Cells. You can purchase Fuel Cells in the e or find them scat- d throughout the et. As you collect e tools, you can ss new parts of s that you have dy explored and ver more cells. Use Fuel Cell Compass d them.

030

It pays to return to areas that you have already explored. Sometimes you'll find Fuel Cells that weren't there before or that you might have missed.

Once you have all of the Fuel Cells you need, climb into the Arwing and take off for another adventure.

Go to Dragon Rock pg. 116

CAPE CLAW

While you were away from Cape Claw, the SharpClaws built a barricade in front of Ocean Force Point Temple. Before you can enter the temple, you must destroy the blocking planks.

CHECKLIST
- [ ] Use a SharpClaw Cannon to break into a cave and Ocean Force Point Temple.
- [ ] Enter the temple to return the SpellStone to its rightful place.
- • NEXT: Explore Ocean Force Point Temple

182 SEIZE THE CANNON

SharpClaws have erected a rickety wooden barricade at the entra[nce] the temple. You'll need firepower to blow away the blockade. En[ter] cave near Queen CloudRunner's former cell. Open the Portal Door, extinguish a fire, then take control over the SharpClaw cannon. A single cannonball blast will provide enough power to knock out the barricade.

Once you have the means to open [the] Portal Door, you can make your w[ay to] the cannon above the beach. Afte[r you] take control over the cannon, tra[in the] sights on the Ocean Force Point T[emple] entrance.

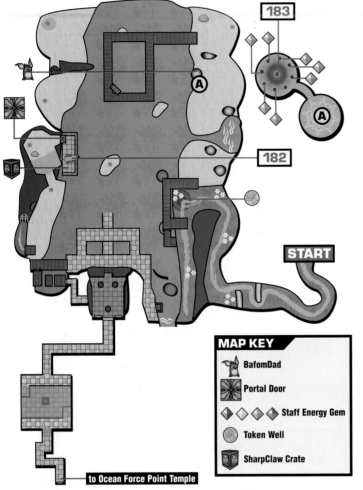

MAP KEY
- BafomDad
- Portal Door
- Staff Energy Gem
- Token Well
- SharpClaw Crate

START

to Ocean Force Point Temple

183 CRASH INTO A CAVE

Before you take off for the temple, turn the cannon toward the beach and hit the huge rock near the pier. Step away from the cannon and swim across the beach to investigate the rubble. You'll find a BafomDad and a hole that leads to a staff energy upgrade.

Destroy the huge rock w[ith] cannon fire, then swim t[o the] beach to collect a Bafom[Dad] and upgrade the energy-[storing] capacity of your staff.

A WALL AND A WELL

You can cause a lot of destruc[tion] with the SharpClaw cannon. If [you] train the cannon on the rock w[all] under the walkway that leads [to] LightFoot Village, you'll blow o[pen] the entrance to a cave. Inside [the] cave, you'll discover a Token W[ell.]

OCEAN FORCE POINT TEMPLE

Ocean Force Point Temple has undergone a few changes since your last visit. The rooms are arranged in the same pattern, but one of the puzzles has been altered.

CHECKLIST

☐ Solve puzzles to make your way into the depths of the temple.

☐ Put the final SpellStone in its place.

• NEXT: Fly back to the Walled City

ONCE MORE INTO THE DEEP

You'll enter Ocean Force Point Temple the same way you entered it the first time. Make your way to the secluded beach, climb two ladders and place the SpellStone in the keyhole.

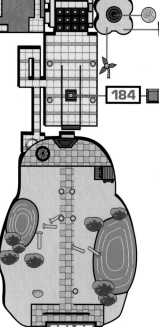

185

184

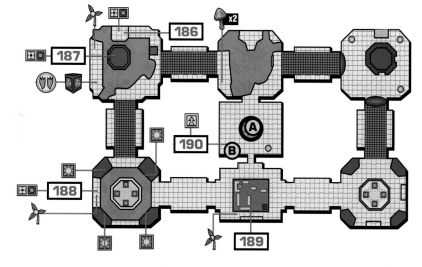

186 x2

187

190 A B

188

189

191

x2

B

START

184 TURN OFF THE POWER

You'll find more electric panels on your second visit to the temple than you saw on your first visit. Have Tricky stay on a pressure plate to reveal the pattern of electric panels that are safe to stand on, then stand on the right panels to turn off the rows, one at a time.

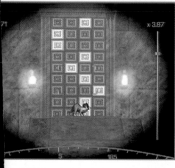

MAP KEY

🐾	BafomDad	🚀	Rocket Boost Pad
🍄	Blue GrubTub Fungus	📦	SharpClaw Crate
🪙	Token Well	👹	SharpClaw Disguise Pad
✴️	Fire Blast Switch	🌀	Magic Plant
✴️	Portal Door	🔷	Staff Energy Gem
⬛	Pressure Plate	🔘	Staff Switch

WATER WELL

After a quick swim, you'll find a Portal Door. Open the door to discover a few helpful items and a well.

Swim down the same tunnel as before, climb up to the Warp Pad and warp to the next section of the temple.

186 BLOCK BOOST

Once you work your way around to a big block on a ledge, push the block to the base of a higher ledge and use it to climb up to the top. You'll find a lever-activated switch on your new perch. Hit it to make a huge circular door roll out of the way.

187 RAISE THE WATER

Explore the outer ledge of the room and break a box to reveal a SharpClaw Disguise Pad. Switch to your SharpClaw guise and st on the pad to make a door on th room's central structure drop. You'll find a switch. After you h the switch, the water level in t room will rise, giving you acces to the next area.

188 COLOR-CODED DOUSING

In the room with the turntable and the Krazoa Statues, you will once again extinguish the flames by making the statues spill water onto the turntable's torches. The variation in the puzzle is that you must match Krazoas with torches of the same color.

You'll have only a few minutes to douse all four torches. The Krazoa Statues and the torches are color-coded. Hit the Fire Blast Switches to make the statues extinguish their matching torches. The turntable speeds up as you extinguish the flames. Be sure to hit the switches in time so that the water pours onto the quickly moving torches.

SHOOT AND SLIDE

mechanics of the block-sliding puzzle are the same as they were
our first visit to the temple, but the path to the trigger point is
tly more complex. Climb
wall and look down at the
le to formulate a plan of
k. While you're on the
ledge, you can pick up a
to energize your Fire
er, too.

Hit the targets on the side of the block to make it slide around the maze. Start by
hitting the block twice while you move around the pit clockwise.

Move around the pit counterclockwise four the final four shots. When the block is
in place, the electricity on the ledges above will shut off.

ROCKET UP AND RUN AROUND

Return to the first room in the area and
Rocket-Boost up to the ledge, then
work your way around the ducts and
cross a bridge to the Warp Pad.

191 THE LAST SPELLSTONE IN PLACE

Warp to the blue-tinted room where you deposited the first
three SpellStones and put the final SpellStone in its place. Mission accomplished! Now, you're really making progress.

SING SPIRIT

though all of the SpellStones are in place, the planet has not
d itself back together. Talk to Queen EarthWalker. She'll tell you
back to the Walled City for a missing Krazoa Spirit.

STOP WALLED CITY RETURN

Go to Walled City pg. 111

Return to the Arwing and
take off on another flight.
You've almost collected
all of the pieces of the
puzzle. One more adven-
ture in the Walled City
should do the trick.

KRAZOA PALACE

Instead of landing on Dinosaur Planet and warping to Krazoa Palace, you will fly directly to the roof of the palace, where you will start your search for a place to release the Krazoa Spirit.

CHECKLIST

- [ ] Release the Krazoa Spirit.
- [ ] Warp to an encounter with General Scales.
- [ ] Collect the Krazoa Spirit.
- [ ] Release the final spirit.

NEXT: Fly to the final fight

DROP AND EXPLORE

From the Arwing's landing spot, run to the far end of the roof look for a hole that you can drop into. After you fall, you'll land o

highest floor of the palace. Jump into the center of the open chamber and drop down one floor. Explore the floor for a passage that leads down to a wind lift-occupied gap. Cross the gap and continue on to a courtyard. There, you'll find a place to release the spirit.

After you drop down a hole from the roof, jump into the open chamber and dro another floor, then look for an open passage.

Cross over a wind lift and continue to a courtyard where you will find the face Krazoa Spirit.

207 RELEASE THE SPIRIT

Stand on the pad in front the spirit statue and pre the A Button. The spirit v leave you, fly through the statue and find its place the palace.

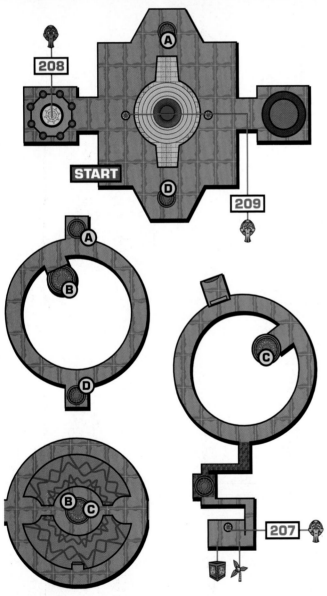

208

START

209

MAP KEY

🗿 Krazoa Spirit

📦 SharpClaw Crate

🗿 Release Krazoa Spirit

🌱 Magic Plant

TURN TO THE ROOF

e you've released the final spirit, turn around and return to the . When you reach the highest floor, look for a wind lift that will ch you to the top of the palace.

Cross over the wind lift again, jump into the middle of the huge chamber and rise to the top floor. Look for a wind lift ride to the roof.

NERAL MAYHEM

hen you reach the stage, General Scales will appear. What rts as a fight will quickly turn into a scene in which Scales ll tell you about his plans to take over Dinosaur Planet. He ll then release a Krazoa Spirit. The spirit will possess you.

But the war is not over yet.

General Scales will start to face off with you in battle, then he will release a Krazoa Spirit and disappear.

208 WARP TO THE FINAL STAGE

When you return to the roof, you will find a Warp Pad that was previously blocked by a force field. Take the warp to a large room and use a ladder to climb up to a stagelike platform.

Run to the Warp Pad on the roof and use it to reach a large room with a stage in the middle. Walk around the stage and look for a ladder to climb.

209 THE LAST SPIRIT RETURNS

When you get back to the roof, you'll find a place to put the last spirit. Releasing the spirit will set off a chain of events that will end with Krystal out of her cage and the ultimate enemy out of his disguise.

You will regret this...

STOP FLY TO THE FINAL FIGHT

I am reborn! The mighty Krazoa God! [laugh]

With the last spirit in place, you have one last battle to win. You'll return to the skies and face off with Andross.

Go to the final fight pg. 124

DARKICE MINES

FLY THROUGH 3 GOLD RINGS TO REACH DARKICE MINES

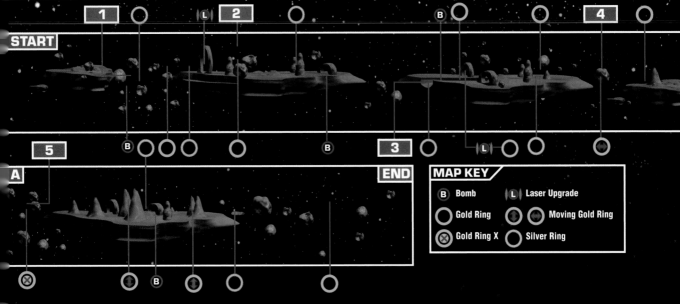

MAP KEY

B	Bomb	**L**	Laser Upgrade
◯	Gold Ring	◉	Moving Gold Ring
⊗	Gold Ring X	◯	Silver Ring

1 STEER AROUND BIG ROCKS

You can blast small asteroids out of your path, but you've got to fly out of the way of the larger rocks. As you zigzag around the floating masses, drift to the left and collect the first Gold Ring.

2 THREAD THE NEEDLE

On your approach to the second Gold Ring, stay to the left and fly through a rock formation to collect a power-up, then aim for a second formation and press X to slow down. You'll find the ring on the other side of the rocks.

3 SPACE TRENCH

Midway through your flight, you'll find a ditch dug into one of the huge asteroids. Fly through the ditch to collect a Silver Ring, a power-up and a Gold Ring.

4 WILY RING

The fifth Gold Ring moves left and r[...] Try to pick up on its movement from [...] distance and lock onto it, zigzagging [...] you fly.

5 TRIPLE TAKE

Near the end of the run, you'll encounter three Gold Rings in quick succession. They will start with a ring that you must shoot through before you can collect it. The others are near rock formations. Fly around the rocks and zone in on the rings.

DARKICE MINES

A dispute between the GateKeeper, who lives in SnowHorn Wastes, and his daughter has led to the imprisonment of a group of SnowHorns in and around DarkIce Mines. As you search for the SpellStone, you will also help the SnowHorns escape and you'll get some help from them in return.

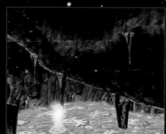

DARKICE MINES: SURFACE

The SnowHorn GateKeeper has sent you to DarkIce Mines in search of a SpellStone. In addition to the precious stone, you will find a group of imprisoned pachyderms in a world of ice and lava. Your journey begins in a fire-filled cave.

CHECKLIST

- [ ] Free the shackled SnowHorn and collect the Bridge Cog.
- [ ] Use the Bridge Cog to extend the bridge.
- [ ] Save the fallen SnowHorn from SharpClaws.
- [ ] Feed Alpine Roots to the SnowHorn and break through the main gates.
- [ ] Blast barriers and SharpClaws with the cannon.
- [ ] Collect three Bridge Cogs and extend another bridge.
- [ ] Find the Dino Summon Horn and ride the SnowHorn through the blizzard.
- [ ] Ride a Jet Bike into the mines.

NEXT: Explore the mines

COME OUT OF THE CAVERN

The two paths that originate from the Arwing's landing spot both reach to the surface of the DarkIce Mines area. As you make your way to the open air, exercise caution so that you don't fall into the fire, but have faith in Fox when you get to the short gaps in the path. He will jump automatically.

Flaming globs of lava pop from the pool. Watch their movement and avoid contact with them as you run along the narrow path.

As you advance, chunks of the hardened lava path will give way and fall into the fire, creating short gaps. Don't let your exposure to the bubbling bath slow you down. Run up to the breaks in the path and let Fox jump across them.

MEET THE MAMMOTHS

SharpClaws and their SnowHorn prisoners populate the sm settlement on the surface. Fight off the guards and speak to t prisoners. One of the massive creatures needs your help.

Can you help me get free?

The SnowHorn near the snow-blocked building is locked in le shackles. If you can free the beast from her bonds, she may be able to help you reach the area beyond the settlement. If only you had a key . . .

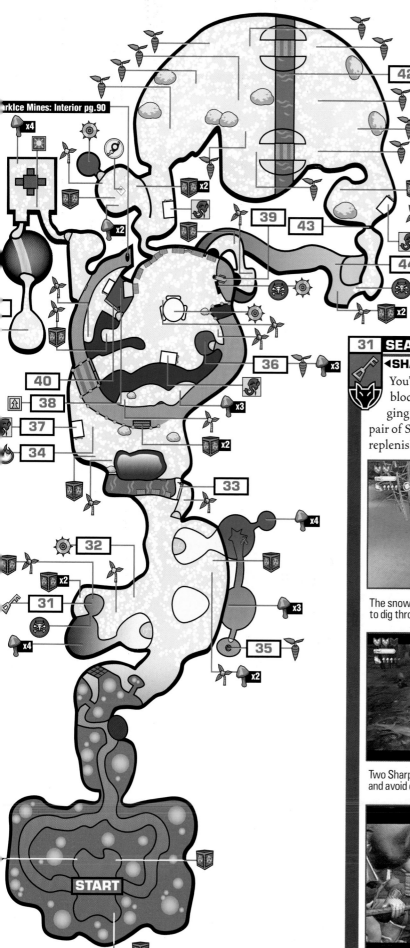

DarkIce Mines: Interior pg.90

MAP KEY

Alpine Root	Life-Force Door
Blue GrubTub Fungus	Rocket Boost Pad
Bridge Cog	SnowHorn Pad
Dinosaur Horn	SharpClaw Basket
Dino Summon Pad	SharpClaw Crate
Fire Blast Switch	Magic Plant
Flame Command	Shackle Key

42
39
43
44
x2
36 x3
40
38 x3
37
34 x2
33
32 x4
x2
31 x3
35
x4 x2

START

31 SEARCH FOR THE SHACKLE KEY

◄SHACKLE KEY

You'll discover that there is a crack in the snow barrier that blocks the entrance to one of the buildings. Use Tricky's digging ability to create a tunnel into the structure and fight off a pair of SharpClaws for a prize. Collect Blue GrubTubs and energy-replenishing items along the way.

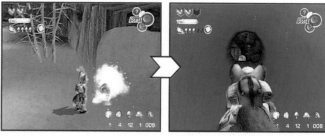

The snowdrift at the entrance to one of the buildings is cracked. Call on Tricky to dig through the snow at the crack and create a tunnel into the structure.

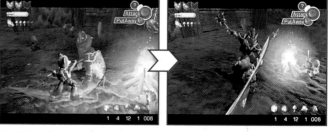

Two SharpClaws warm themselves at the fire. Fight them off, one at a time, and avoid contact with the flames.

Victory against the SharpClaw guards will give you access to a room that holds the Shackle Key. Use the staff to free the key from its box, then grab the item and continue your quest.

32 EXCHANGE THE KEY FOR A COG
◀BRIDGE COG

SnowHorns can store helpful items in their trunks. When you return to the shackled SnowHorn and use the Shackle Key to free her, she will give you the item that she was keeping from the SharpClaws. If you have already explored the area at the base of the waterfall, you know exactly where the Bridge Cog belongs.

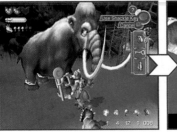

This might be of use to you. I found it whilst I was working.

33 MECHANISM MAINTENANCE

With the Bridge Cog in hand, climb down, or jump, into the river make your way to the mechanism under the waterfall. Place the into the space between the other cogs and pull the lever. A bridge extend from one side of the river to the other.

34 FLAME FOR TRICKY
◀FLAME COMMAND

After you cross the bridge, you'll discover a downed SnowHorn surrounded by SharpClaw attackers. Defeat the bad beasts and talk to the SnowHorn. The wise mammoth will encourage Tricky to practice his fire-spitting Flame Command.

When you approach the SharpClaws, they will break away from the SnowHorn and go after Fox. Hit them each with a fast and furious Staff attack. You'll win the battle with ease.

Go on, youngster, give it a go.

The exhausted SnowHorn will tell you that he is too weak to help, but he will give Tricky words of encouragement. Your young charge will then have the wherewithal to learn the Flame Command on the spot.

FEED YOUR FRIEND

SnowHorns need a lot of food to stay healthy. The migh mammoth that you saved from the SharpClaws will tell yo that if he had nourishment, he could help you advance.

.. you through the main gates. I need some food.

If the downed SnowHorn were so weak from hunger, he could bash open the gates to the nex area. Before you can move on, you must bring him two Alpine Roots.

FIRE AND ICE IN THE SNOWHORN SETTLEMENT

search for Alpine Roots takes you
to the settlement. An ice barrier
ks one of the structures. Use Tricky's
e Command to melt the barrier, then
a fire inside the structure and let the
oor break apart. You'll gain access to
e below the building.

Break into the ice-blocked building by instructing Tricky to use his Flame Command. Melt the floor and break through to an underground chamber that holds a buried Alpine Root.

On your way out of the underground chamber, push the massive ice block through the narrow passage into a position over the grate. Then climb onto the block to get out of the hole.

A ROOT IN THE RAVINE

ks roll down the ravine that borders the next area. Drop into the
e and run toward the source of the boulder barrage. You'll dis-
r a cave that is blocked by ice. Use Tricky to melt the ice and
re the cave for an Alpine Root.

Run against the flow of boulders and look for an ice-covered cave. Use your well-fed sidekick to break the ice and dig for SnowHorn food.

37 CATCH A RIDE

With two Alpine Roots in hand, return to the fallen SnowHorn. The food will give him energy to stand up and give you a ride. Climb the nearby platform and hop onto the beast.

After you feed the SnowHorn, climb up to the center of the nearby platform and press the A Button to jump onto the mammoth's back. Guide the creature to the gate and press A again to have the SnowHorn break through.

CANNON QUEST

nemy fires cannonballs
a high perch in the
pClaw fortress. Use Tricky
reak into an ice-covered
el, then follow the path to
annon. On the way, you'll
he Rocket Boost to reach a
ledge and you'll run along
rrow wooden path while
onballs fall around you.

The tunnel leads to a wooden structure and a cave. Climb, fight and use your staff's Rocket Boost to reach another wooden path.

By following the rickety path along the side of the cliff, you will reach the SharpClaw Cannon. Defeat the operator of the cannon and take control over the powerful device. You can swivel the cannon and adjust the power of its blasts. Fire on the SharpClaw forces that emerge from the building and break through a wooden barrier that blocks the entrance to a tunnel. When all of the guards are gone, you will have access to the SharpClaw structure and to a cave that is directly below the cannon.

Five SharpClaws emerge from the building below. Pick off all of the creatures with the cannon to gain access to the building and to the cave below the cannon.

A wooden barrie blocks a tunnel the other side of the fortress. Bla the barrier with cannon fire.

SEARCH THE COMPOUND FOR COGS

The absence of enemies in the area will give you the freedom to explore the entire compound. Enter the structure at the center of the fortress and collect a cog.

The cave below the cannon was blocked by a Life-Force Door. With the SharpClaws gone, you can enter the cave and find another Bridge Cog.

GO BEYOND THE COMPOUND

The tunnel that was blocked by a wooden barrier leads to an area side the compound. Once there, you will find an icy path that lea another ice-covered cave. Melt the barrier and search the cave third Bridge Cog.

Climb up to the formerly blocked tu and run up a slope on the other side Melt an ice barrier and collect a Bri Cog in a cave.

40 BUILD A BRIDGE

On your way to the cannon, you passed a mechanism that was missing three cogs. Return to the mechanism and put the cogs in their places, then pull the lever. A new bridge will extend to an unexplored area on the other side of the ravine.

CROSS AND CRAWL

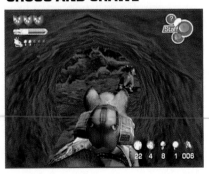

On the other side of the bridg you will find a cave that is bl by dirt. Make sure that Tricky enough energy to follow you commands, then instruct him dig a tunnel into the cave.

41 LIGHT AND LEAP

◄DINOSAUR HORN

You'll find a furnace and a blocked passage in the cave. When you hit a switch on the wall with a Fire Blast projectile, a timer will start to tick down. Use Tricky to light the furnace in the allotted time to open the passage.

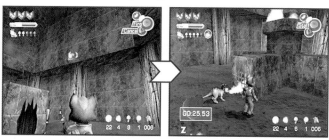

Hit the projectile switch on the wall with a Fire Blast to trigger a timer. As the timer counts down, instruct Tricky to light the furnace's four openings. When the furnace is lit, the barrier will fall.

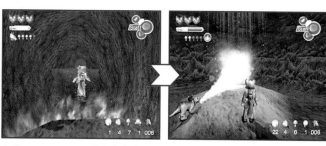

In the next room, you'll find a ledge on the other side of a wide gap. Take a leap of faith toward the faraway ledge. You'll land safely on an invisible path. Follow the path to the Dinosaur Horn.

42 CALL FOR A RIDE

Return to the area where you found the third Bridge Cog and use the Dinosaur Horn on the pad that is decorated with a horn carving. A SnowHorn will answer the call.

Use the Dinosaur Horn on a carved pad to call for a SnowHorn. Climb aboard the beast and guide him into a blinding blizzard, collecting Alpine Roots along the way.

After you follow the trail of Alpine Roots, head for the two torches to reach shelter from the storm. If you stray from the Alpine Root path, your SnowHorn will lose energy and you will lose your way.

43 CRASH INTO A CAVE

Tricky will disappear after you emerge from the storm. With your sidekick gone, you'll need help from the SnowHorn to break into an ice-blocked cave.

DEFEAT THE DINOS AND BLAST OFF

You'll find a pair of SharpClaw Guards in the cave. Defeat them to make a Life-Force Door dissolve, then hop onto their Jet Bike and go for a high-speed ride.

44 SOAR THROUGH THE SHAFT

Your Jet Bike journey will take you through some territory that you have already explored by foot, then into the depths of DarkIce Mines. The bike flies at a good clip, and you can even increase the speed a little by pressing and holding the A Button. When you enter the mines, keep your eyes open for staff energy gems and pick them up as you go. When you get to the end of the path, you'll fly off the bike, onto a conveyor belt.

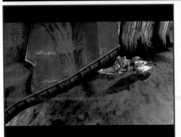

CHECKLIST

- [ ] Collect the Silver SharpClaw Prison Key.
- [ ] Collect the Gold SharpClaw Prison Key.
- [ ] Journey to the lowest level of the mine.
- [ ] Climb the DarkIce Mines Towers.
- [ ] Save the SnowHorn from the two SharpClaws and use him to break into the boss room.
- [ ] Fight Boss Galdon.

• NEXT: Return to Dinosaur Planet

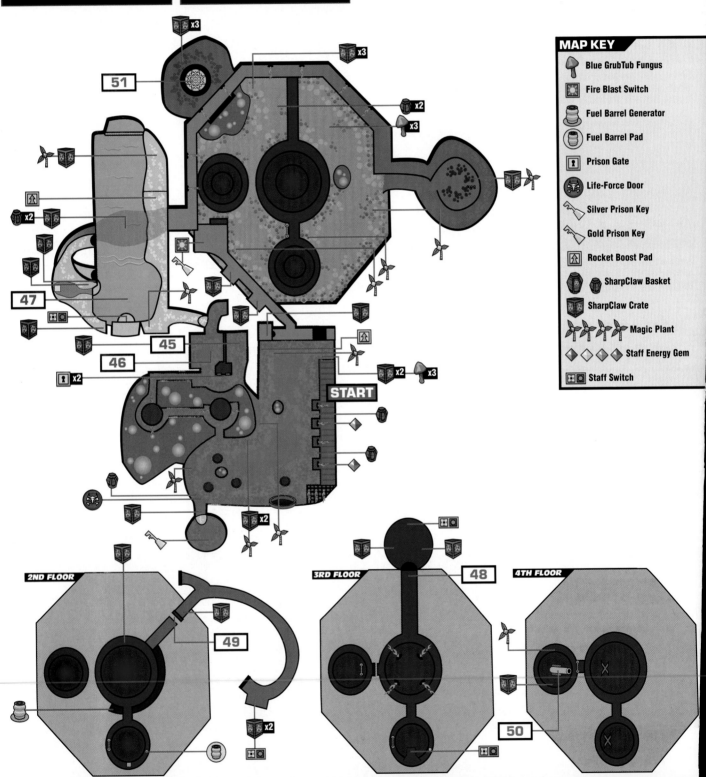

MAP KEY

- Blue GrubTub Fungus
- Fire Blast Switch
- Fuel Barrel Generator
- Fuel Barrel Pad
- Prison Gate
- Life-Force Door
- Silver Prison Key
- Gold Prison Key
- Rocket Boost Pad
- SharpClaw Basket
- SharpClaw Crate
- Magic Plant
- Staff Energy Gem
- Staff Switch

51

47

45

46

START

2ND FLOOR

49

3RD FLOOR

48

4TH FLOOR

50

45 ENTER THE PRISON, FIND A KEY
◄SILVER PRISON KEY

After you survive a ride on the conveyor belt, search for a Rocket Boost Pad. Boost up, then crawl through a narrow passage to an area where you will discover a key on the other side of a fiery barrier.

Run from the flames on the conveyor, then drop off at an opening. Fight SharpClaws and search the area for a Rocket Boost Pad. Fly up onto a ledge and look for a small tunnel on the right.

Crawl through the tunnel to a place where huge snowballs roll past small alcoves. A flame protects one of the alcoves. Shut off the flame by hitting a Fire Blast Switch, then collect the Silver Prison Cell Key. Use the key to save Tricky.

AVE BELINA TE

Use the Gold Prison Cell Key to open the cell that is adjacent to the room where you found Tricky. You'll find Belina Te, daughter of the SnowHorn GateKeeper. After a short conversation with Belina Te, the mammoth will crash through a wall to another part of the mines, leaving a pile of rocks in her path.

Once you talk to Belina Te, she will find her own way to a different section of the mine, and Tricky will discover a hidden passage. Have Tricky dig a tunnel and follow him to the other side.

46 SAVE PRINCE TRICKY
◄GOLD PRISON KEY

With the Silver Prison Cell Key in hand, return to the main mine area and cross a fire-protected path to a pair of prison cells. Save Tricky from the cell on the right and guide him to a meltable ice barrier.

Fight off the SharpClaws in the main mine area, then cross the lava pit. On your way over the pit, you'll deal with two dangerous rotating flame jets.

When you reach the cells, use the key to unlock the cell on the right to save Tricky. Return to the open area, defeat any straggling enemies and use Tricky to melt a barrier that protects the Gold Prison Cell Key.

47 CROSS THE POND

When you reach the cavern that has a deep pool, look up and fire on three green icicles. The icicles will drop into the water and float, giving you a path to a switch. Hit the switch to bring forth ice floes and a passage to another area.

Focus your Fire Blast on three green icicles that hang from the ceiling. When the icicles drop, hop onto them and cross the water to a switch. Cross the water again and take a path to the area above the waterfall.

Jump onto the moving ice floes and leap to a ledge on the other side. You'll discover a huge ice cube that you can push into the water, creating a platform that extends the path to an unexplored area.

CATCH UP WITH BELINA TE

On the path to the lowest part of DarkIce Mines, you'll have to pass through a series of conveyor belts with fire jets that turn on and off. When you reach the bottom, you'll find Belina Te. Search the floor for a ladder up to a spiral walkway.

48 CARRY A BARREL TO A BARRIER ABOVE

You'll find a tall tower in the middle of the mine area. There is a cracked wall near the top of the tower. You must find a way to take a Fuel Barrel up to the wall and blast open a passage. Climb a ladder up to a path where barrels roll down at a constant rate. Pick up a Fuel Barrel at the beginning of the path and avoid the rolling barrels. Since they all follow the same path, look for safe areas. Leave the Fuel Barrel on a pad, then climb up and activate a mechanism that will lift the barrel to your level.

After you survive the rolling barrels, leave the SharpClaw Barrel on a pad, climb up and turn on a mechanism that will deliver the barrel to you.

Pick up the Fuel Barrel and carry it past a series of flame jets to the cracked wall. Blast the wall and hit a switch that will activate a bridge.

49 MAKE A PATH TO THE CANNON

Cross the new bridge, near the origin of the rolling barrels, and follow the flow of rolling snowballs to a switch. Hit the switch to create a new bridge near the top of the tower. Climb up and cross to the cannon. After you break through the wall and hit the switch near the top of the tower, you'll be able to cross a bridge near the middle of the tower. On the other side of the bridge, follow the path down to another switch. By hitting it, you'll open up a bridge near the top of the tower. Climb up and continue to the SharpClaw Cannon.

50 BLAST AND BUILD

After you defeat the operator, take control of the SharpClaw Cannon and train it on two boarded-up switches. Hit each switch to trigger the creation of half of a lava bridge.

As you hit each of two switches with cannon fire, you will see solid lava rise from a pool near the base of the tower. The two formations will create a bridge.

BOSS GALDON

51 | WARP TO BOSS GALDON

The two bridges that you created with cannon shots give you access to a room with a warp pad. Warp to the boss room, stun some Blue GrubTubs and prepare for a battle.

EAT THE TAIL AND BE EATEN

Frightening Boss Galdon will destroy Fox if you fight it face-to-face. Run to the back of the beast and have Tricky stay to draw the boss's eye, and hit the boss's tail when it flashes. The boss will swallow Fox whole. Once in the stomach, hit the hanging blob with the staff.

As the battle begins, run under the boss to its other side, and attack its flashing tail. When the boss gobbles up Fox, target the hanging blob in the stomach.

THAW OUT THE BOSS

The big beast who rules over the mine and the SpellStone hibernates in ice. You must wake it to take its prize. Tell Tricky to train his flame on the ice formation and step back as the boss breaks free.

As much as you might like to keep the boss on ice, you must thaw it out to take back its SpellStone. Hit the ice with Tricky's flame and prepare for a large-scale battle.

FINISH HIM
◄SPELLSTONE

After several hits to the stomach blob, the boss will spit out Fox. Aim your Fire Blast at a slit in the boss's chest. The boss will gobble up Fox again. Hit the blob several times more and collect the SpellStone as it drops.

After you escape the boss's stomach, you'll see a slit in its chest. Aim for the chest when it opens up and wait to be swallowed again. Another victory in the stomach will earn you the SpellStone.

TOP | LAST WORDS

Following your battle with the boss, Belina Te will thank you for freeing the SnowHorns from their enslavement in DarkIce Mines. The SpellStone is yours and the SnowHorns are liberated. You'll return to the warp ring and prepare for another adventure on Dinosaur Planet.

 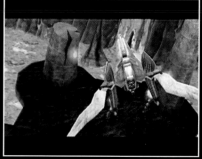

Together you can lead the SnowHorn Tribe ...

Return to Dinosaur Planet pg. 40

FLY TO
CLOUDRUNNER FORTRESS

FLY THROUGH 5 GOLD RINGS TO REACH CLOUDRUNNER FORTRESS

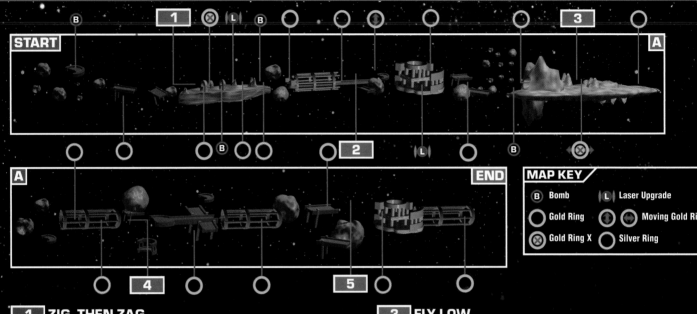

MAP KEY

Ⓑ Bomb		Ⓛ Laser Upgrade	
⬤ Gold Ring		⬍/⬌ Moving Gold Ri	
⊗ Gold Ring X		◯ Silver Ring	

1 ZIG, THEN ZAG

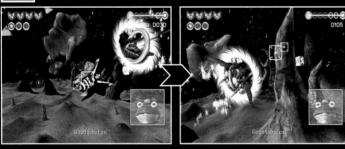

Rock formations surround the first two Gold Rings. Fly to the right to grab the first ring, then slow down, veer to the left, fire through the second ring and collect it, too. Then turn sharply to the right to collect a laser upgrade.

2 BLAST AND MOVE

After you emerge from the first tunnel, use a bomb to clear away the large group of approaching enemies, then close in on the vertically moving fourth Gold Ring.

3 FLY LOW

As you fly over the purple landscap you'll see a blocked ring moving to left and right. Use a bomb or spin through enemies to clear the way. Watch the ring's movement carefull and pluck it out of the sky.

4 CORKSCREW ATTACK

Spin as you emerge from the second tunnel, drop under the large structur collect a Gold Ring, then slow down, rise up and enter the next tunnel to c lect another ring.

5 TIGHT TURN

You'll find the ninth Gold Ring on the side of the area. After you collect i past the round structure then turn sharply to the right. Enter the tunne go for the last ring.

CLOUDRUNNER FORTRESS

Over the course of your CloudRunner Fortress adventure, you'll travel on the surface of the water and on structures high in the sky. Since Scales and his army attacked the fortress and imprisoned its occupants, much of the building is in ruins. As you explore the structure, you will have to find your way around large chunks of rubble and cross massive gaps.

CLOUDRUNNER FORTRESS

Rescue of the Winged Runners

CLOUDRUNNER FORTRESS

CloudRunner Fortress has become a prison under the control of General Scales. You must break into the prison, then break out with the CloudRunners. You'll find a useful disguise along the way.

CHECKLIST

- [ ] Hop through an obstacle course and fire on a switch to open the main gate.
- [ ] Climb the tower, open a gate and confront General Scales.
- [ ] Break out of the prison and get the SharpClaw Disguise.
- [ ] Retrieve your staff and free the prisoners.
- [ ] Collect three Light Gems and bring power to the wind lifts.

• NEXT: Go to the fortress roof

90 | HOP THROUGH HOOPS

The CloudRunner Fortress Main Gate is locked. Climb down to the obstacle course in the water and swim over to a pressure plate. Rings of magic will appear under the arches. Run the course and hop through all three rings before time runs out. A Fire Blast switch will appear above the gate.

Climb down to the water and swim to the pressure plate on the other side of the bridge. Your weight on the plate will trigger the beginning of a tightly timed obstacle course. Start hopping toward the first arch.

Run through the course quickly but carefully. If you fall into the water, you can swim through the hoops, but it'll take more time. After you make your way through the last hoop, a switch will appear above the gate. Hit it with a Fire Blast.

UPWARD SPIRAL

A spiral walkway leads to the top of a tall tower. As you run up the walkway, watch out for the floating robots and try to avoid their damaging electrical attacks by hiding behind the pillars.

91 | SEARCH FOR A SWITCH

You'll find a ladder at the top of the spiral. Slide down and search area for a wall switch. After you hit the switch, a gate on the s walkway will open. Climb up and over to the new opening.

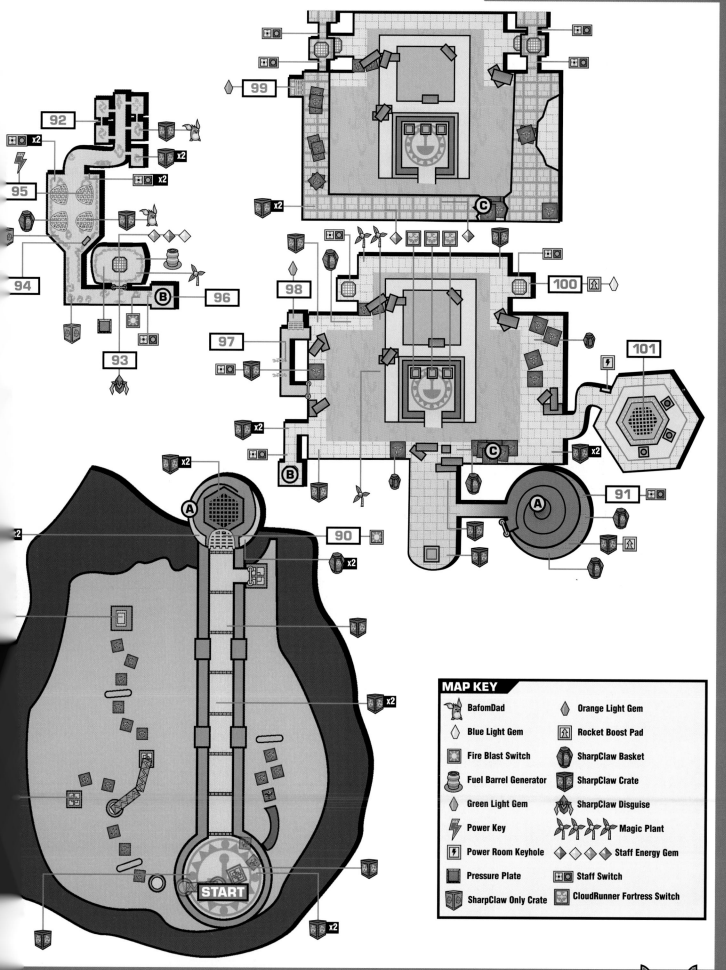

MAP KEY

- BafomDad
- Blue Light Gem
- Fire Blast Switch
- Fuel Barrel Generator
- Green Light Gem
- Power Key
- Power Room Keyhole
- Pressure Plate
- SharpClaw Only Crate
- Orange Light Gem
- Rocket Boost Pad
- SharpClaw Basket
- SharpClaw Crate
- SharpClaw Disguise
- Magic Plant
- Staff Energy Gem
- Staff Switch
- CloudRunner Fortress Switch

TROUBLE AT THE TOP

General Scales has captured the Queen CloudRunner, and he has his sights set on Fox McCloud. Unfortunately, your trail will lead you right to the leader of the SharpClaws and his electrically charged robots. A quick confrontation will lead to captivity in one of Scales's prison cells. Scales has won the battle, but he won't win the war.

I do not know what you're talking about.

You will tell me . Where can I find the fox.

92 JAIL BREAK

No staff, no key, no problem—you can get out of the cell in a hurry. Find a dark rock on the cell's light wall, face it, press the A Button and push. You'll move the rock easily and gain passage to the adjacent room.

TIPTOE THROUGH THE PRISON

Grab the key, but don't wake the Sharpclaw.

A tunnel leads to a chamber containing CloudRunners in cages and a sleeping guard. Walk along the wall, far from the guard, and pass through the doorway to the next area. Don't attempt to capture your staff just yet. You'll wake the guard if you get too close.

CONTACT THE CREW
93 ◀SHARPCLAW DISGUISE

Climb down into the room with the massive circular grate and use an explosive barrel to blow a hole into the ceiling. Exposing the air above will allow you to radio your crew. When you make contact, Slippy will tell you about a new discovery—the SharpClaw disguise.

Place the explosive barrel on the circular grate and stand on the pressure plate to activate the fan. The barrel will float to the ceiling and explode, creating a hole that will allow you to establish radio contact with your crew.

CARRY WITH THE CLAW

You can lift some objects only if you are disguised as a SharpClaw. Pick up and t SharpClaw boxes to collect their contents. Do the same with SharpClaw Fuel Barrels to cause an explosion.

94 BE THE GUARD

Wearing the SharpClaw disguise, return to the CloudRunr cages. The guard will leave, allowing you to take his post. C lect your staff after he leaves and use it to open the cages.

SET THEM FREE, GET A KEY
◄POWER GENERATOR KEY
There are four switches on the wall. One of the switches will free an old BoneHead who will tell you to activate the wind lifts and give you the Power Generator Key.

◗CLIMB THE WALL
the key in hand, return to the main hall and hit a switch to open oor to a room with brick walls. Get a good grip and climb up to a ge at the top disguised as a SharpClaw to avoid enemy fire.

TRIGGER AND RUN
◄GREEN LIGHT GEM
Three switches in the center of the courtyard open three gates. Press the left switch to expose the Green Light Gem, then collect it before the gate closes.

ou'll find three ornate switches by climbing a ramp to an area in the center of he courtyard. Hit the switch on the left to open a gate that will give you ccess to the Green Light Gem.

un across the courtyard disguised as a SharpClaw to avoid electrical shocks rom the floating robots. Climb the ladder, run down the hall and claim your rize.

LIBERATE THE PRISONERS
Hit the other switches to open the other cages. One of them holds another CloudRunner. The others hold helpful items—a Scarab and a BafomDad—and one of the prison cells contains a BafomDad.

97 PREPARE FOR LIGHT GEM COLLECTION
You'll find three Light Gem behind gates in the courtyard area. Before you attempt to collect the first Light Gem, hit a switch to drop a ladder and put out fires with your Freeze Blast.

99 UP AND AROUND
◄ORANGE LIGHT GEM
You'll find the Orange Light Gem in an alcove above the courtyard. Hit the center switch, climb boxes to the next level and run to the stone before the gate drops.

The center switch opens a gate that gives you access to the Orange Light Gem. After you hit the switch, turn around and climb a pile of boxes to the upper level.

There are SharpClaw guards on the upper level, but you don't have time to fight them. Use your SharpClaw disguise to slip past them unnoticed then run to the stone.

◄BLUE LIGHT GEM

SF

The Blue Light Gem is high above the courtyard. You can reach it with your Rocket Boost. Hit the right switch to open the gate, then run and boost.

Freeze the flame that blocks the Blue Light Gem's area. Then hit the switch to open the gate, run into the alley and boost before the gate closes. The last of the Light Gem will be yours.

The Power Generator Room is in a corner of the courtya Once you have collected all three Light Gems, use the Pow Generator Key to enter the room. Then put each stone in its proper place quickly, as the room is full of poisonous gas. The generator will bring power to the wind lifts and give you access to another area of the fortress.

CLOUDRUNNER FORTRESS

You have escaped from the fortress prison but the queen is still captive and her children are being chased by SharpClaws. Before you can find the SpellStone, you must help the royal family.

Only she can help you find the SpellStone.

CHECKLIST

☐ Rescue Queen CloudRunner.

☐ Save the CloudRunner children.

☐ Battle on bikes for the SpellStone.

NEXT: Return to Dinosaur Planet

The sprawling upper reaches of CloudRunner Fortress are crawling with SharpClaws. Switch to the SharpClaw disguise and stand on a pad to open a gate, then sweep through the dock area and take out SharpClaw guards.

In the guise of a SharpClaw, you can pick up a barrel and carry it to a pad in a ro machine will lift the barrel and transport it to the next floor while you climb t der to follow it up.

After the machine takes the barrel to the upper floor, pick up the barrel, take side and toss it across a gap to blow away a wooden barricade.

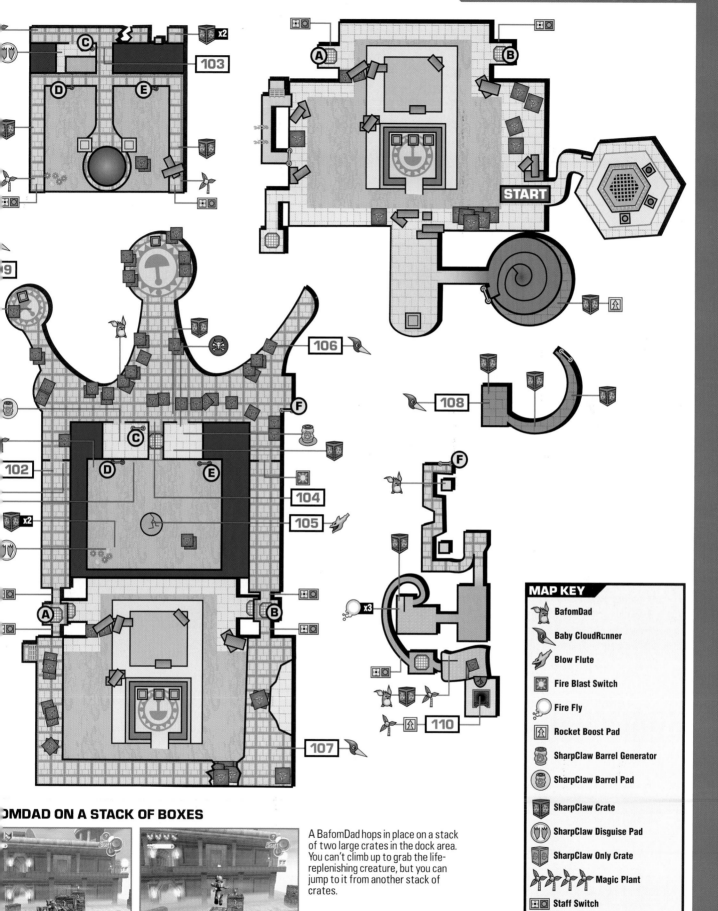

103

x2

START

106

108

102

104

105

107

110

x3

x2

MAP KEY

	BafomDad
	Baby CloudRunner
	Blow Flute
	Fire Blast Switch
	Fire Fly
	Rocket Boost Pad
	SharpClaw Barrel Generator
	SharpClaw Barrel Pad
	SharpClaw Crate
	SharpClaw Disguise Pad
	SharpClaw Only Crate
	Magic Plant
	Staff Switch

OMDAD ON A STACK OF BOXES

A BafomDad hops in place on a stack of two large crates in the dock area. You can't climb up to grab the life-replenishing creature, but you can jump to it from another stack of crates.

CLIMB UP TO THE QUEEN

After you break through the barrier, you'll drop into another courtyard. Defeat the SharpClaws in the area and stand on a glowing pad, in disguise, to make a ladder drop. Climb the ladder to find the queen in a cage.

A CLUE FROM THE QUEEN

When you talk to the queen through the bars of her cage, she will tell you that the floor of her cage is weak. All you need is something to destroy the column under the cage to set her free.

---

104 TWO SWITCHES, ONE GATE

There is a switch on either side of the ledge that rings the courtyard. You'll be able to reach one of them easily. The way to the other one is blocked by debris. Jump from the ledge onto a stack of crates, then jump back to the ledge that is on the other side of the debris. After you hit both switches, you will be able to open a gate on the floor below.

106 CLOUDRUNNER ON A CRATE

After you leave the courtyard, you'll see a lone SharpClaw trying to reach up to a small CloudRunner on a stack of crates.

Defeat the enemy with a staff attack, climb up to the CloudRunner and play the flute. The young flier will leave the crate to find its mother.

---

105 CRACK THE COLUMN

◀ CLOUDRUNNER FLUTE

The courtyard gateway gives you clear access to the room the explosive barrel. Grab the barrel, take it across a win and use it to destroy the column under the cage.

Grab the explosive barrel and take it to the wind lift. Toss the barrel into wind, then jump across the gap. You may have to push the barrel to the o side while you're in the air.

Destroy the column under the queen's cage with the explosive barrel. Af the queen escapes, she will give you the CloudRunner Flute and ask you t save her four children.

107 RUN TO THE RESCUE

Following the first CloudRunner rescue, you'll see the location o second CloudRunner child. Run down a long hall, hit a switch to a gate, take on two SharpClaws and play the flute.

DROP AND BOOST

hird child is on the other side of a solid wall. Drop down from the site of the
d rescue, make your way through the broken pieces of a wall and find a
t Boost Pad off the spiral path.

t up to a natural rock ledge and take on a group of three SharpClaws. After
attle, the third CloudRunner child will hover near you. Play the flute to send
ild away.

EXPLODE INTO THE TREASURE ROOM

need an explosive barrel to break
the inner chamber of the treasure
. Pick up a barrel from the barrel gen-
r and throw it into the closest wind
Make your way to the treasure cham-
reverse the flow of the wind lift to
the barrel drop and use it to destroy
eak wall.

Throw an explosive barrel into the wind lift, then quickly make your way around to the entrance of the treasure chamber and keep running to the bottom of the wind lift.

Get the SpellStone out of here!

Reverse the flow of air at the bottom of the wind lift to make the barrel drop. Disguise yourself as a SharpClaw, pick up the barrel and use the FireFly Lantern to find a weak wall. After you blast the wall, you'll be on your way to the inner sanctum.

BUMPER BIKES
◄SPELLSTONE

ou'll take on three SharpClaws on Jet Bikes for possession of the second
pellStone. Your goal is to ram the opposing bikes and put them out of com-
nission. You'll win the SpellStone after you take care of the last bike. Avoid
bstacles, hit turbo tiles and take on the SharpClaws one at a time.

109 FINAL RESCUE

The last CloudRunner child is not far from where you found the first one. When you reach the final flier, you'll take on four SharpClaw attackers. Fight them off as quickly as you can, play the flute and seek out the Queen CloudRunner. She'll open the door to a hidden treasure room.

Scales has hidden the SpellStone inside the treasure rooms.

STOP TO THE TEMPLE

 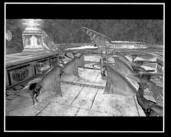

... you need to find the Ocean Force Point Temple.

Before you take off for Dinosaur Planet again, you'll meet with the Queen CloudRunner. She will tell you to seek out the Ocean Force Point Temple, the SpellStone's rightful place. Your adventures will continue with a battle on the beach.

Go to Dinosaur Planet pg. 56

FLY TO
WALLED CITY
FLY THROUGH 7 GOLD RING TO REACH CLOUDRUNNER FORTRESS

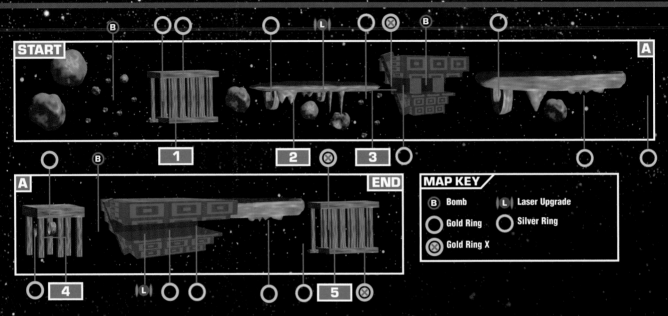

START

A

1   **2**   ⊗   **3**

A   **END**

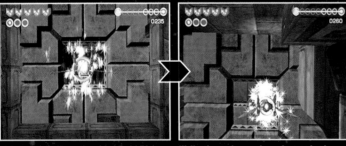

4   ⊥   **5**   ⊗

MAP KEY

Ⓑ **Bomb**	Ⓛ **Laser Upgrade**
◯ **Gold Ring**	◯ **Silver Ring**
⊗ **Gold Ring X**	

1   COLUMN CONTROL

Fly into the open structure at the beginning of your run and move around the columns. You'll find the first Gold Ring between two of the stone posts.

2   GO BELOW

Fly under the huge, flat rock and make your way through a hole to collect the second Gold Ring. Then make a tight to the right and grab a Laser upgrade

3   BRAKE AND BOOST

After you collect the third Gold Ring, you'll fly through a series of portals that open and close. Use the X and Y Buttons to adjust your speed and fly through the portals while their doors are open.

4   RINGS INSIDE OF RINGS

You'll reach the fifth and sixth rings in quick succession. Both rings are in the middle of ring-shaped stone openings. After you grab the fifth ring, turn ha the left and collect the sixth ring.

5   BIG FINISH

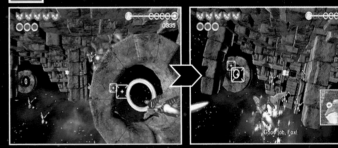

The last two Gold Rings are blocked You'll have to shoot through them before you can collect them. Fly through the ninth ring, veer to the le into the big structure, then move to the middle and grab the last ring.

WALLED CITY

You'll visit the land of the Sun and Moon Temples twice—first to collect a SpellStone, then later to collect a Krazoa Spirit. You'll receive advice from Tricky's father, King EarthWalker, on both visits, and you'll find four valuable keys over the course of your Walled City adventures: the Gold and Silver Teeth and the Sun and Moon Stones.

WALLED CITY

The RedEye Tribe rules over the ancient Walled City. To get the city's SpellStone, you must find a way to conquer the tribe and collect its sacred keys.

TROUBLE WITH A CAPITAL T

The T. rex patrols that guard the Walled City will attack if you get too close. You can try to fend them off with Fire Blast shots, but you won't do much damage. If a dinosaur engages you, press the B Button to break away from the battle, and run.

147 SUNSHINE

The only way to get to the underground cell of King EarthWalker is to light the Sun and Moon Beacons. Shake the tile near the Sun Beacon with a Ground Quake to make it rise. Then enter the main temple, find passage to the beacon and light it with Tricky's Flame.

The Sun Beacon is in a small structure close to the main temple. After you shake the ground switch with a Ground Quake, the beacon will rise from the structure and your attention will shift to an opening in the main temple.

Climb the outside of the main temple and enter the passage marked with two orange flames. Follow the passage to the top of the Sun Beacon structure and use Tricky to light the beacon before time runs out.

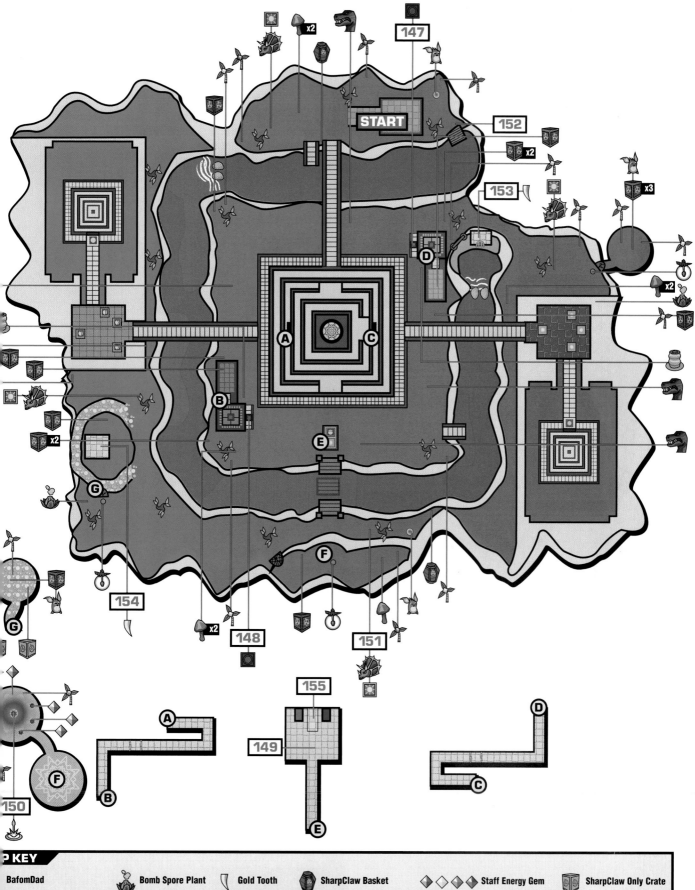

START

147
152
153
154
148
155
149
150
151

A
B
C
D
E
F
G

KEY

BafomDad	Bomb Spore Plant	Gold Tooth	SharpClaw Basket	Staff Energy Gem	SharpClaw Only Crate
Blue GrubTub Fungus	EarthWalkers	Moon Switch	SharpClaw Crate	Sun Switch	Super Ground Quake
Bomb Spore Planting Patch	Fire Blast Switch	Silver Tooth	Magic Plant	T. rex	

148 MOONBEAM

Day is the best time to light the Sun Beacon, and night is the best time to light the Moon Beacon. Locate the crescent tile near the Moon Beacon structure and hit it with a Ground Quake. Enter the main temple, go underground, surface and light the beacon.

After you shake the tile nea the Moon Beacon structure the Moon Beacon will rise a you will see an opening framed by blue torches at t main temple.

Run to the main temple and enter the blue torch passage. As you make your way through the passage, be sure to avoid the damaging blasts.

After you have l both the Sun and Moon Beacons, you will have access to the underground pas sage that leads King EarthWalke cell.

149 FAMILY REUNION

Enter the underground chamber to reunite Prince Tricky with King EarthWalker and get a clue from the king about the location of the third SpellStone.

Tricky my son, you don't have to worry about me ..

King Earthwalker is hidden away in an underground chamber. After you witness the father-son reunion and talk to the king about the SpellStone, he will point in the direction of a helpful staff upgrade and trigger the appearance of a new bridge that spans the river.

150 EARTHQUAKE UPGRADE
◄ SUPER GROUND QUAKE

Cross the wooden bridge opposite the king's chamber an Tricky to burn away blocking thorns. Climb a wall, then Bomb Spore to blast your way to an upgrade.

You have collected the GROUND QUAKE!

Tricky earns his GrubTubs. Have H burn away a barrier, then climb u Bomb Spore Planting Patch and open a hole in the ground. Drop in the hole and upgrade your Groun Quake for the power to knock la creatures off their feet.

151 TORCHLIGHT TRAIL

After you climb down from where you found the upgrade, talk to the EarthWalker nearby and aim your Fire Blaster at a switch in a tree to restore fire to a torch.

RIVER WALK

An EarthWalker on the shore will tell you that the secret of the river can be fo the leaves. Hit the switch in the EarthWalker's tree to light another torch.

MOTE WALKER

...hind the structure that holds the Sun Beacon to find your way around a small ...e. You'll find another Earthwalker and a Fire Blast Switch that lights a torch.

FIRE AND WATER

You'll find another EarthWalker near the Arwing. Talk to the dinosaur, then hit the switch in the nearby tree. After all four switch-torch connections are made, a special event will take place in the water.

2 WATER RING RACE

...e river plays host to a water race with magic rings as check-...ints. Dive into the water at the waterfall near the Arwing and ...rt swimming. Every time you make your way through a magic ...g, you'll get more time on the timer. If you hop through the ...t hoop before time expires, you'll gain entrance into a building ...the small ravine.

Leap off the plank near the waterfall, line yourself up with the closest ring and make sure that Tricky is behind you. Swim straight through the first two rings, then drift left to the wall as you approach the third ring and the next waterfall.

After you go over the waterfall, you'll have a chance to run on solid ground, but you'll make better time if you stay in the water and let the current carry you. Zigzag around two land masses as you approach the bridge.

After you swim under the bridge, drift to the right and run on the land. Before you dive back into the water, line yourself up with the left side of the next ring.

When you hit the shallow water section, you'll have no option but to run. Aim for the right side of the next ring as you go.

Aim for the left side of the deep water ring. If you have 12 seconds or more remaining after you swim through the ring, you'll be in good shape. Swim to the shallow water, then make a run for the final ring. Drop into the ravine and run to the open building.

153 TAKE THE TOOTH

◀SILVER TOOTH KEY ⬛⬛⬛

Following your ring race around the river, you will gain entrance into a small building in the ravine, where you will collect one of two dinosaur teeth.

155 A BOSS WITH BITE

With both teeth in hand, return to King EarthWalker and place the objects in the mouths of two fierce-looking statues. The path to a toothy boss battle will open up.

BOSS REDEYE

T. REX ROAMS THE UNDERGROUND

You'll need a lot of firepower to beat the huge RedEye boss under the temple. Use electricity to knock the beast to the ground, then hit him with explosives.

Shoot a Fire Blast Switch to open a cage in the corner, then pick up a Fuel Barrel. Step on a pressure plate to trigger an electrical surge in the hallway as the RedEye approaches.

The electricity will knock the RedEye to the ground. Toss the barrel at the beast's head, then turn, run and hide in an alcove before he stands and continues his hallway patrol.

154 RULE OVER THE REDEYES

◀GOLD TOOTH KEY ⬛⬛⬛

The upgraded Ground Quake gives you the power to k[...] over RedEyes. Shake them to the ground, then fight t[...] with barrels or blasts for the Gold Tooth.

Approach the massive RedEyes and knock them to the ground with the upgraded Ground Quake. You can hit them with Fuel Barrels, Fire Blasts or [...] Blasts to knock them out.

After all RedEyes are gone, a Life-Force Door that blocks a structure on [...] other side of the river will disappear. Go there to capture the Gold Tooth.

FINISH OFF THE FIEND

◀SPELLSTONE ⬛⬛⬛

Every time you shock the boss and hit him with explo[...] the pressure plates will move closer to the electricity's so[...] The last time the beast falls, he will drop at your feet.

After you shock the RedEye and hit him with explosives a total of four ti[...] you'll beat him for good and earn the third SpellStone.

STOP A NEW ADVENTURE

With another victory to your nam[...] you will return to the Arwing, accompanied by Tricky and King EarthWalker. The king will stay t[...] protect the Walled City, but you must return to Dinosaur Planet a[...] place the SpellStone in the Volca[...] Force Point Temple.

Go to Dinosaur Planet pg 68

ALLED CITY

final SpellStone is in place, but you must find the last Krazoa
t before you can bring all of Dinosaur Planet's satellites back
ther. You'll find a passage to the spirit in the Walled City.

CHECKLIST

- [ ] Collect the Sun Stone from the Sun Temple.
- [ ] Collect the Moon Stone from the Moon Temple.
- [ ] Put the Sun and Moon Stones into their places in the main temple.
- [ ] Warp to the Krazoa Shrine.

• NEXT: Take the Krazoa Test of Knowledge

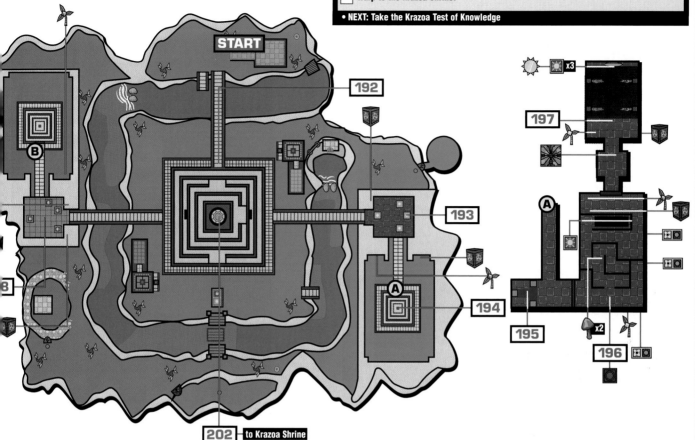

START

192

197

193

A

194

195

196

A

202 → to Krazoa Shrine

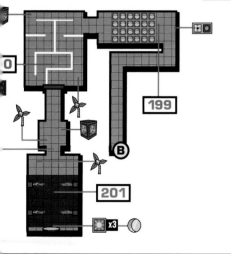

199

B

201

x3

KEY

Blue GrubTub Fungus   Magic Plant

Fire Blast Switch   Staff Switch

Moon Stone   Sun Stone

Portal Door   Super Ground Quake Switch

SharpClaw Crate

192   A CONVERSATION WITH THE KING

You'll find King EarthWalker waiting
for you on your return to the Walled
City. He will point out that two new
areas have opened since you last vis-
ited the city. By exploring the new
areas, you will discover how to make
your way to the Krazoa Spirit. Your
first stop should be the Sun Temple.

193 BLOCK OUT THE SUN

Near the entrance of the Sun Temple, you'll find a pit that features four big blocks and four sun holograms. You must slide the blocks into the holograms. The paths burned on the floor of the pit show where you can slide the blocks. You'll have to put some of the blocks in place before you slide the other blocks. The puzzle will reset if any blocks hit the pit's outer wall. Once all of the blocks are in place, a new puzzle at the top of the temple will present itself.

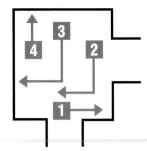

Slide the blocks into place as shown on the d gram, in the indicated order. The first block th you put into place will stop the second block hitting the wall. The second block will act as stopper for the third block.

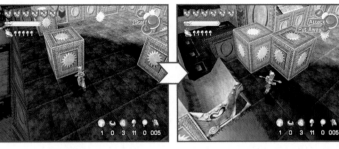

Slide the blocks along the paths that are burned into the pit floor. You'll have to use some of the blocks in combination to make the puzzle work out.

After the last block slides into place, an iris will open on top of the temple, se up the next puzzle.

194 ZOOM THROUGH THE CIRCLE

Use an elevator platform to rise up to the top of the temple, then stand on the center tile and look through the circular opening with the Hi-Def Display Device. After you zoom in to the distant wall, the door to the Sun Temple will open.

195 SHOW THEIR FACES

You'll find three blocks that fit into holes on the ends of a T-sh track. When you examine the blocks, you'll notice that each one symbol on one side. Move the blocks along the track and rearr them so their symbols show when they are placed in the holes.

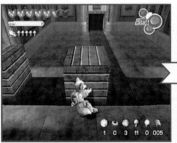

Pull the blocks out of their p and move them to different so the symbols on their face show. After you put the last into its new place, an area or other end of the room will o

SWITCH MAZE

u'll find a switch at the ginning of a maze. Use the ound Quake on the switch start a timer and open a door the other side of the maze. t switches to make invisible rriers disappear and open ssages as you run through e maze.

Use the Ground Quake on the switch at the beginning of the maze to start a timer and open a passage. You'll find another switch around the corner. Hit it to open another passage.

The third switch in the series is covered by fire. Douse the flame with an Ice Blast, hit the switch and move on to the edge of a deep pit. Hit a Fire Blast switch on the other side of the pit to open the path to a bramble-covered button. Tell Tricky to burn away the brambles, then hit the switch and continue on to a Portal Door at the end of the maze.

TAKE THE SHOT
SUN STONE

After you open the Portal Door, you'll find a large disk on the other side of a gap. Fire switches through the holes in the disk to trigger the appearance of a path to the Sun Stone.

Open the Portal Door, hit the Fire Blast Switches in clockwise order around the large spinng disk, starting with the one on the left. A path to the stone will appear.

198 MOON SHADOWS

Moving on to the Moon Temple, you'll find another block-sliding puzzle in the temple courtyard. Shadowy lines on the ground reveal the paths that the blocks should take as you push them into place.

You'll push three of the blocks directly into their places, then use the blocks as stoppers while you push the fourth block along a crooked path on the ground.

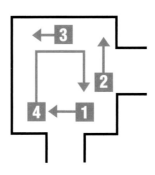

The diagram shows the recommended order and paths for pushing the blocks into place. Move blocks 1, 2 and 3 first so you can push the fourth block off them and into place. If the first three blocks aren't in place when you move the fourth one, you'll risk sliding it out of the puzzle area.

TILE TRAIL

r you look through the round hole at op of the temple with the Hi-Def Dis-Device, you'll gain entry to the temple rior. There, you'll hit a switch to open r and make blocking gates move up down. As you make your way through gates, move methodically from tile to o avoid dropping with falling tiles.

200 ROCK AND WANDER

Use Ground Quake while standing on the raised tile in the center of the large Moon Temple chamber to cause a timer to start ticking down and a door to open. Navigate a maze of invisible walls and make your way to the doorway before time expires. You'll have the greatest success in the invisible maze if you start by moving away from the doorway, then work your way around the room in a clockwise pattern.

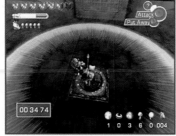

If you hit an invisible wall, you'll see traces of the wall for a few moments. Make a mental note of where you saw the wall, then look for a different route to the open passage.

201 SHOOT THE MOON
◄ MOON STONE

A giant disk rotates on the other side of a wide gap. Hit Fire Blast Switch they are exposed by a hole in the disk. A path that leads across the gap t Moon Stone will appear after you hit the last switch.

202 TAKE IT TO THE TOP

Return to King EarthWalker's former cell and put the stones i same statues that hold the Gold and Silver Teeth. The top of the temple will rise to reveal a Warp Pad.

KRAZOA TEST OF KNOWLEDGE

Your journey to the last Krazoa Spirit is a wind and fire obstacle course over impossibly deep pits. When you reach the spirit, he will test your memory of past adventures.

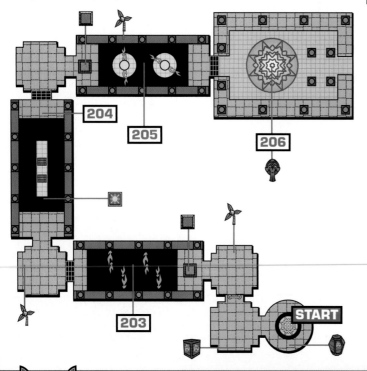

CHECKLIST
- [ ] Survive an obstacle course to reach the Krazoa Spirit.
- [ ] Take the Krazoa Test of Knowledge.
- NEXT: Set a course for Dinosaur Planet

203 FLY THROUGH FIRE

The first obstacle on the way to the Krazoa test is a pit filled w series of wind lifts and flame jets. Stand on a pressure plate to o gate, then float over the pit and try to avoid the flames.

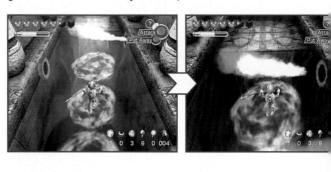

MAP KEY
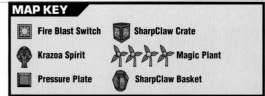

Fire Blast Switch		SharpClaw Crate	
Krazoa Spirit		Magic Plant	
Pressure Plate		SharpClaw Basket	

204 | ICE AND FIRE

After you cross through a wind lift to a solid path in the next pit, use Ice Blasts to extinguish blocking flames. Cross to the other side and shoot the Fire Blast switch to open the gate.

205 | TURNING TERROR

The fire and wind theme continues in the third long chamber. Stand on a pressure plate to open the gate on the other side of the room, then fly through a wind lift to a platform that holds rotating flames. Run around the platform to avoid the flames, then cross over to another platform and repeat the process.

Fly over to a round platform and move quickly to avoid rotating flame jets, then fly to the next platform and avoid another pair of flames.

06 | MEMORY GAME

The Krazoa Spirit will ask you to place six items in front of holographic images of the areas where you found them. Look around the room before you talk to the spirit and identify the areas, then initiate the test. After you put an item in its correct place, a flame will rise to indicate a successful match. For example, place the Totem piece in front of the LightFoot Village image and the Dinosaur Horn in front of the SnowHorn Wastes picture. Try to remember each match, in case you have to try again.

Place the CloudRunner Horn in front of the image of the domed building and the meteor before an image of a space scene.

Place the MoonSeed in front of a moonscape with a crater, and the Gold Tooth in front of an image of the Walled City.

OP | RETURN TO DINOSAUR PLANET

After the Krazoa Spirit possesses you, you will find yourself back in the Walled City. Make your way to the Arwing and take off for Dinosaur Planet. You'll fly directly to Krazoa Palace.

To Dinosaur Planet pg. 80

FLY TO
DRAGON ROCK

FLY THROUGH 10 GOLD RINGS TO REACH DRAGON ROCK

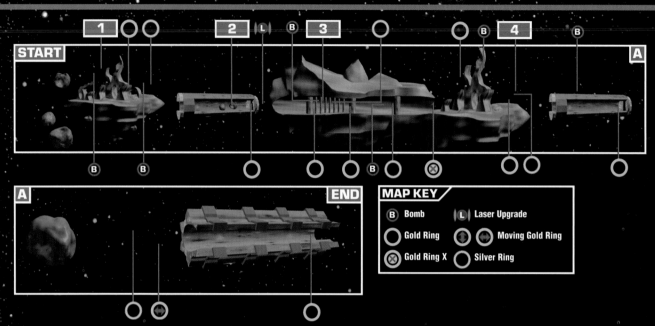

START

1 ○○ **2** L B **3** ○ ○ B **4** ○ **A**

B B ○ ○ ○ B ○ ⊗ ○○ ○

A ... **END**

MAP KEY

B	Bomb	L	Laser Upgrade
○	Gold Ring	🔵	Moving Gold Ring
⊗	Gold Ring X	○	Silver Ring

○ 🔵 ○

1 GRAB THE BOMB AND GLIDE

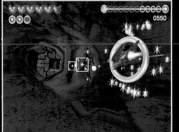

Collect the bomb power-up and shoot it into the tunnel to clear the mines and asteroids in your path.

2 BANK AND BOOST

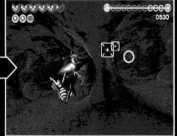

After you collect the second Gold Ring, you'll approach a narrow, vertical op- ing. Spin on your way out of the tunnel to avoid enemy fire, then fly through t small, square opening. Use your boost or brake as necessary.

3 GOLD RING SLALOM

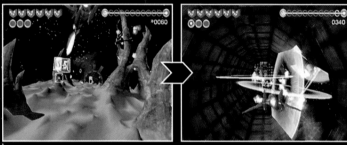

Swing first to the left to hit a Gold Ring and grab a bomb then immediately right to snag another gold ring. Keep firing while you swerve back to the left and through the opening.

4 PICK UP A RING AND A BOMB IN ONE TURN

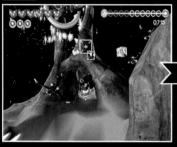

After you emerge from the tunnel the end of the run, fly up to collec ring in front of the rock formation, swoop down to collect a power-u then level out before you collect t second-to-last ring and enter the tunnel.

The hostile land of Dragon Rock is a prison for members of several Dinosaur Planet tribes, and an electrically powered headquarters for the army of General Scales. During your adventure on Dragon Rock, you'll save and befriend three different dinosaurs and use them to work your way into the core of Dragon Rock. There, you'll fight a demonlike creature for the final SpellStone.

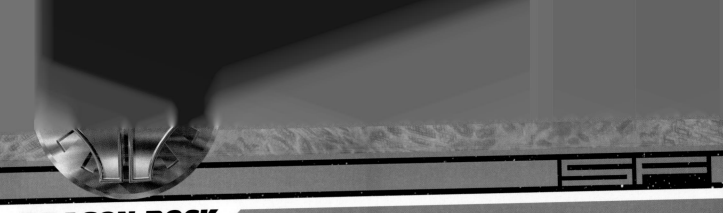

DRAGON ROCK

Hovering robots patrol the red desert landscape of Dragon Rock, and a large collection of traps protects the enemy-controlled buildings. You'll need help from several friends to find the area's SpellStone.

CHECKLIST

☐ Break into High Top Tower and activate a switch to free an EarthWalker.

☐ Use the EarthWalker to break four power generators.

☐ Once the generators are gone, fire on the hovering robots to open a gate.

☐ Free a High Top and protect the creature while he opens another gate.

☐ Search for Krystal's CloudRunner and look for a way to free him.

☐ Use a barrel to break through a barrier and activate mechanisms to free the bird.

☐ Ride the CloudRunner around the compound and destroy the four spires.

☐ Defeat Boss Drakor.

• **NEXT:** Return to Dinosaur Planet

173 INFILTRATE HIGH TOP TOWER

As soon as you land, scan the landscape and look for the large, imposing High Top Tower. As you approach the building, you'll discover a

ladder that is protected by flame jets. Climb up the ladder and run along the ledge. You'll find a board-blocked entrance and more flame jets. You'll also find a barrel pad and a switch, which activates a barrel-grabbing device. It looks like the makings of a barrel-transporting puzzle!

Head for the big building in the distance and climb the ladder. Avoid the dangerous flames. When you get to the top, run along the ledge and look for a way to break through the wooden barrier.

174 BREAK INTO THE BUILDING

You can break through the wooden barrier at the top of the ladder using the barrel at the far end of the ledge. The trick is to get the barrel over to the barrier. Set the barrel on a barrel-shaped pad and activate the barrel-grabbing device. Stand on floor panels to shut off flame jets as the device carries the barrel to a higher area.

The only way to get the barrel up to a ledge is by using a barrel-carrying device. Rest the barrel on a pad and hit a switch to activate the device.

Follow the barrel as it floats over the path and stand on floor panels to cut off flame jets temporarily. After the device releases the barrel, pick up the explosive container and throw it at the wooden barrier.

175 FREE AN EARTHWALKER

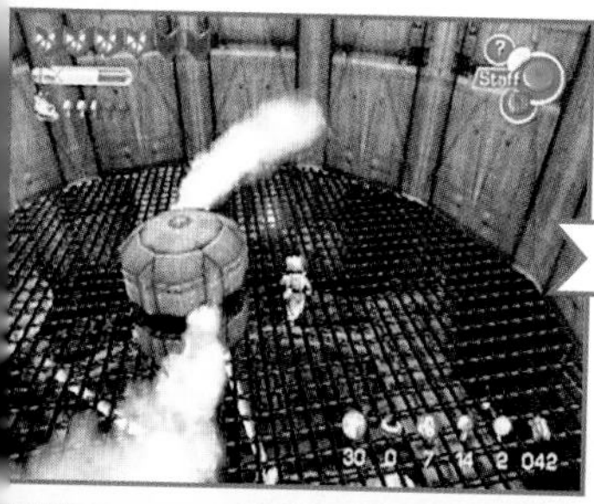

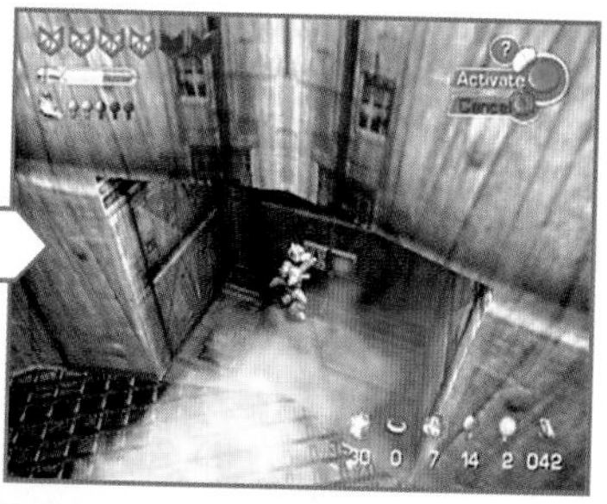

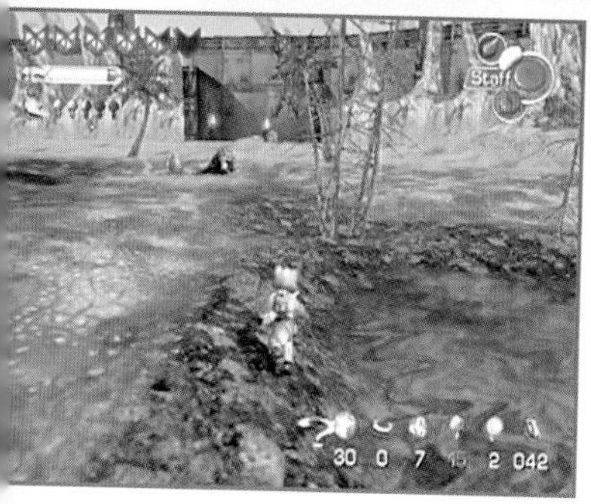

The rotating, flame-spewing device in the center of the round room protects a small alcove. Circle the room, duck into the alcove and hit a switch to make a gate in another building drop, freeing an EarthWalker. Climb down from the tower and search for the dinosaur.

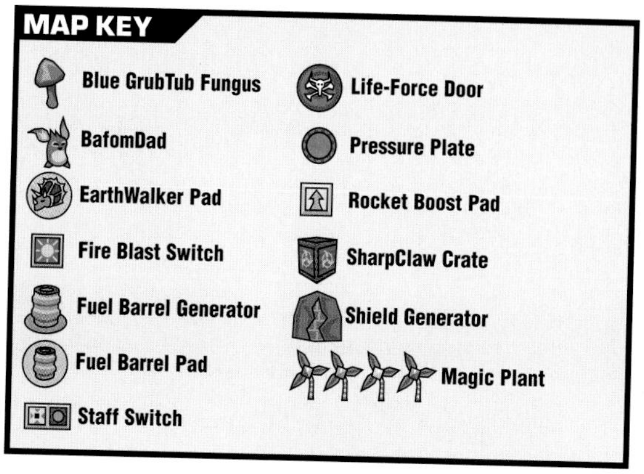

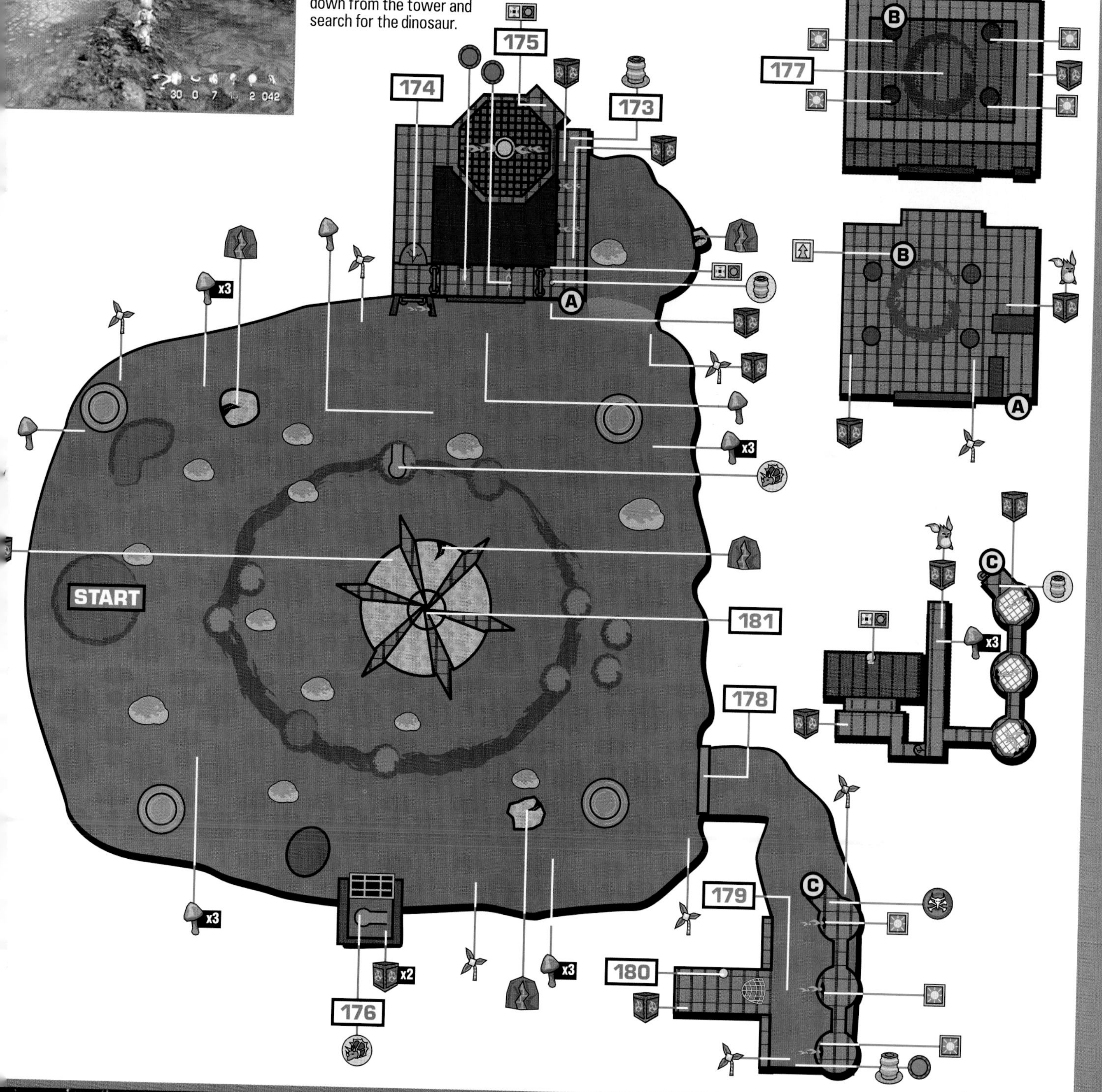

MAP KEY

Blue GrubTub Fungus		Life-Force Door	
BafomDad		Pressure Plate	
EarthWalker Pad		Rocket Boost Pad	
Fire Blast Switch		SharpClaw Crate	
Fuel Barrel Generator		Shield Generator	
Fuel Barrel Pad		Magic Plant	
Staff Switch			

175

174

173

177

A

B

x3

x3

x3

START

181

178

C

x3

179

C

180

176

x3

x2

The EarthWalker will tell you about the defenses surrounding the High Top complex. He can help you break into another part of the tower. Jump onto his back and take off.

Now get on my back. Let's do some damage!

The EarthWalker is a big, powerful beast, and he's fast, too—a much more satisfying ride than the lumbering SnowHorn. Hop onto the EarthWalker's back and explore the environment in style.

RETURN TO THE TOWER

The destruction of the generators and robots will cause a tower entrance on the ground floor to open. Enter the building and use a Boost Pad to launch to the ledge.

CUT OFF THE POWER

Four power generators are embedded in rock walls and rock formations. Search the cracks in the rocks for the green, glowing lights of generator control panels, then use the power of the EarthWalker to blast through the cracks and break the panels.

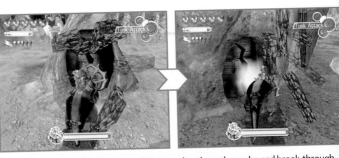

Search the rock surface for green light seeping through cracks and break through the cracks with the EarthWalker.

You'll find a total of four power generators. After you have destroyed them all, the force fields around the floating robots will disappear.

SHOOT THE ROBOT GUNS

Without their force fields, the floating robots are vulnerable to your Fire Blaster shots. Dismount from the EarthWalker, seek out the robots and destroy them. Use the rock formations for cover or strike from a distance to avoid laser fire.

TALK TO THE GENTLE GIANT

As you explore the top ledge, you will work your way around to a face-to-face meeting with a massive dinosaur—a High Top. Talk to him.

I've tried to break these ropes, but they're too strong.

BREAK THE BONDS

High Top is bound by four electric cords. You must destroy the [cords] at their sources to free the dinosaur. The power sources will [regen]erate after a few sec[onds], unless you destroy all [of th]em in a hurry. Aim your [staff] at the Fire Blast [switc]hes near each power [sourc]e.

You'll break the dinosaur's bonds by hitting Fire Blast Switches near the sources of the four cords. If you take too much time, the power sources will regenerate. After you free the High Top, you'll be able to take him for a ride.

SEARCH FOR THE CLOUDRUNNER

[Whe]n the High Top gets to the end of the line, he'll smash a genera[tor a]nd open a huge gate. You'll continue your journey on foot. [Explo]re the new opening and look for a CloudRunner in a cage.

That's what I was looking for.

Explore the ground floor and listen for the cries of the CloudRunner. The CloudRunner needs your help.

MISSILE COMMAND

As you ride on the back of the High Top, you'll encounter several waves of enemy missiles, swarming from a tall tower. The missiles will grow in number as the waves persist. Take out the missiles as soon as they come into view.

Missiles pop out of the tower in large groups. You've got to take them out before they get too close to the High Top.

You'll never run out of firepower as you blast the missiles. Fire into the crowd and try to thin out the swarms as quickly as you can.

FREEZE THE FIRE CRAWLERS

Fire Crawlers run rampant in the warehouse. You won't have any luck hitting them with your staff at first. Use the Ice Blast to freeze them, then knock them out. You have to take out all three of the Fire Crawlers in the area to clear away the Life-Force Door.

179 AIR SUPPORT

The barrel-grabbing device's path runs through three flame jets. You can turn the flame jets off for a few seconds at a time by hitting nearby Fire Blast Switches. Tell Tricky to stay on the floor panel that triggers the device. Follow the device as it carries the barrel and clear the path by turning off the jets.

Shoot the Fire Blast Switches to turn off the flame jets as the device carries the barrel to the top of a ledge.

180 DROP THE CAGE

After you break through the barrier, hit a switch to make the CloudRunner's cage move back and forth, past an inactive flame jet. Return to the ground floor and tell Tricky to light a furnace near the cage. The flame jet above the cage will activate and burn through the rope that holds the cage, causing the cage to drop.

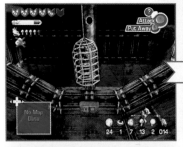 

Hit a switch to make the cage move back and forth, then activate a flame jet that will burn through the rope that suspends the cage. The cage will drop and the CloudRunner will break free.

TUNNEL TROUBLE

You must transport the barrel through three wind tunnels. Wait for the flame in the tunnels to stop for a moment, then toss the barrel across the gap. If the rel doesn't cross the gap, you may have to push it in midair.

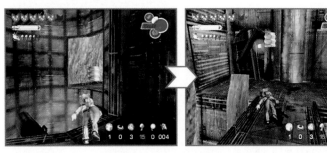

Two flame jets protect the final tunnel. Wait for them both to shut off, then t the barrel. The barrel should float cleanly to the other side. After you make it across the tunnel, pick up the barrel and use it to destroy a barrier.

SPIRE FIRE

Krystal's CloudRunner will take you on a ride around the co pound. You must destroy the four spires and swarms of m siles to gain entrance into the great tower.

Take on the swarms of missiles, then target the spires. It may take a fe tours around the complex for you to complete the task.

OSS DRAKOR

1 FLYING FIRE

...ediately after you knock out the four spires, you'll face Drakor in ...ther fast-firing battle sequence. As the beast zigzags around the ...ns of his arena and flies through fire jets, you must aim carefully ... hit him with a blast barrage. He'll attack you with shots of his ... and leave explosive mines in midair for you to run into. The ...es are high. If you can survive the battle, you'll win the fourth and ...l SpellStone.

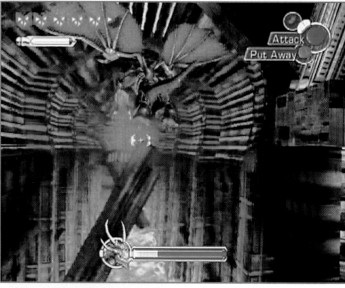

Drakor flies swiftly around his arena. As you follow him, you must unload as many shots as you can in Drakor's direction. Lead with your shots to score direct hits.

...TROY DAMAGING OBSTACLES

...n you see midair mines, fire on them to knock them out of the air. ...can also shut off flame jets by hitting Fire Blast Switches.

REPLENISH YOUR ENERGY

At times, you will find floating power-up boxes. Hit the boxes to produce energy-replenishing items.

DOWN IN FLAMES

◄SPELLSTONE

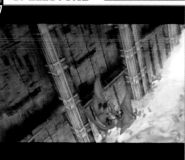

When you finally knock all of the energy out of Drakor, he will sink into the lava and you will earn the last of the SpellStones.

STOP RETURN TRIUMPHANT

Thanks again, Fox.

Once you have collected the SpellStone, you'll say "goodbye" to your new friends and take to the skies for the journey back to Dinosaur Planet. Next stop: Ocean Force Point Temple.

Go to Dinosaur Planet pg. 76

ANDROSS
The Final Fight

Andross!

REVENGE OF THE TYRANT

Although it seems that General Scales is the villain responsible for tearing apart Dinosaur Planet, you'll discover that the real baddie is the evil, floating simian, Andross. He has been disguised as a Krazoa Spirit to fool you, but you'll discover his true identity once you put the last spirit in place. You'll launch to outer space for one final trial—a winner-takes-all battle against the gigantic faces of Andross.

MATCH UP WITH THE MASK

The boss of all bosses shows his Krazoa face to you first. Concentrate your fire on the glowing glass eyes and the diamond-shaped symbol on the boss's forehead and circle around the whirling waves of energy that come out of his mouth. After you destroy all three targets, the creature will spin around and show you his real face.

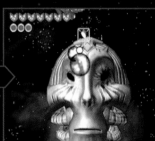

Andross's Krazoa mask fires damaging waves of energy from its mouth. Navigate around the torrents and aim for the mask's three weak points.

FACE OFF WITH THE MONKEY

After you destroy all three of the mask's weak points, the boss will spin around to reveal his real face. The massive monkey uses two hands to grab your ship, and he spits space debris from his mouth. Aim for the diamond-shaped segments of Andross's hands, then blast the space debris, being sure to fly through the Silver Rings among the rocks to replenish some of your energy.

Aim for the monkey's hands when he shows his palms, starting with the one your left. When Andross spits debris from his mouth, fire on the rocks and fl through the Silver Rings.

SPIN AWAY FROM THE SUCTION

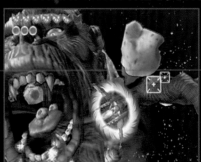

After Andross spits out debr he'll suck in the space junk a try to consume your ship. Fly away from the mouth and sp repeatedly to avoid being pul in. If you are pulled into the mouth, you'll lose energy and battle with the mask will sta again from the beginning.

ONCE MORE AROUND

After you destroy Andross's hands in the first round, you'll fight both the mask and the monkey again. During your second battle with the mask, it will generate enemy ships. In your second battle with the monkey, he'll send waves of damaging energy from his hands. Circle around the waves and aim for the diamonds.

FALCO PITCHES IN

Once you've faced both of Andross's faces twice, your long-lost teammate, Falco, will fly into the screen. He'll introduce power-up boxes to the battle. When you face Andross's waves of debris, you'll find power-ups among the rocks and rings.

BOMBS AWAY

After you collect a bomb, wait for Andross to suck in debris then fire the bomb into his mouth. He'll swallow the explosive, which will detonate inside of him.

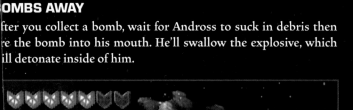

ACQUIRE EXPLOSIVES

When Andross spits out rocks and debris, fire into the cloud of clutter and look for a power-up. After you break the power-up box, you'll see a bomb upgrade. Pick it up.

Keep your eyes open for the power-up box. Break it and collect the bomb inside.

BATTLE THE BRAIN

After Andross swallows the bomb, he'll become transparent, with only his brain exposed. Fire on the brain and avoid the boss's lunging attacks.

THE BATTLE COMES TO AN END

You probably won't beat the brain the first time it is exposed. When Andross encases himself again, collect another bomb, fire it into his mouth and fight the brain again.

END FOX SAVES THE DAY

Once the big brain is completely drained, you will be victorious. The planet will patch itself together, Falco will rejoin the team and Krystal will finally be free of Andross's bonds. The adventures have come to a successful end!

UNLOCK OPTIONS WITH TOKENS

DINOSAUR PLANET HAS A WEALTH OF CHEATS

Every section of Dinosaur Planet has a well, where you can purchase Cheat Tokens. Some wells are hidden. Others are out in the open. After you collect a Token, toss it into the well in the Warp-Stone's Game Well Maze. Half of the Tokens unlock game options. The others give you clue-filled fortunes.

SEARCH FOR WELLS NEAR AND FAR

See page 38

The first well that you will find is located in the ThornTail Hollow Store. After you collect the Small Scarab Bag, toss 20 Scarabs into the well for a Token. Throw it into the maze well to unlock a credit-viewing option.

See page 31

Warp to Ice Mountain and use a Bomb Spore to blast your way into a cave. You'll find a well and a Fuel Cell. The Token that you can purchase from the well will allow you to unlock an option for music sampling.

See page 48

After you pass the floating meteorite in Moon Mountain Pass, use a MoonSeed to reach a Fuel Cell and a well. Buy a Token at the well to unlock a Dinosuar language subtitle option.

See page 76

You can see the adventure in sepia tone after you unlock an option using a Token from Cape Claw. After you take control over the cape's cannon, blast a hole into a cave wall and break through to a well.

See page 39
See page 65

You'll find wells after you ride an ice floe down the river in SnowHorn Wastes and after you rocket up to the ridge that surrounds LightFoot Village. Both give you Tokens that trigger fortunes from the maze well.

See page 69
See page 78

You'll find wells during your second visit to each of the Force Point Temples. Buy Tokens from the wells, then drop them into the maze well for fortune clues about the later stage of game.

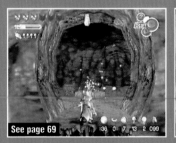

1	Land at Krazoa Palace with Krystal and use a Fuel Barrel to destroy an obstacle.
2	Pick up another barrel from the generator and blow open a door on the lower deck.
3	Climb down a ladder and jump across gaps to a life-replenishing BafomDad.
4	Use a Fuel Barrel inside the palace to destroy a crate barrier.
5	Walk down the hall and open two more doors with Fuel Barrels.
6	Talk to an EarthWalker in the palace to learn about the Krazoa Spirits.
7	Destroy an enemy with a Fuel Barrel to make a Life-Force Door disappear.
8	Step onto a pressure plate to make a gate open, then run through the opening.
9	Take the Krazoa Test of Observation. Find the spirit in the shuffling baskets.
10	Bring the Krazoa Spirit back to Krazoa Palace.
1	Land in ThornTail Hollow with Fox McCloud and search for Krystal's staff.
2	Fight four SharpClaws in front of Queen EarthWalker's home.
3	Upgrade the staff with the Fire Blaster in an underground cave.
4	Use the Fire Blaster to open the door to the queen's home. Talk to her about Tricky.
5	Fire on a Bomb Spore Plant to make it explode, then collect the falling spores.
6	Plant a spore in a planting patch and blast your way into the WarpStone's garden.
7	Collect Scarabs, then buy Rock Candy at the ThornTail Store.
8	Give the Rock Candy to the WarpStone and warp to Ice Mountain.
9	Destroy a box barricade with a Fuel Barrel and fight SharpClaws on the other side.
10	Hit a Fire Blast Switch to open a door to Tricky's cell.
11	When SharpClaws chase Tricky, hop onto a Jet Bike and join the race.
12	After you save Tricky, use his sidekick commands to solve a platform puzzle.
13	Tell Tricky to dig a hole, then tunnel to SnowHorn Wastes.
14	Fight off attacking SharpClaws and learn the Heel command.
15	Use Tricky to dig a hole at the base of a fallen tree. Fall in to upgrade your staff.
16	Collect an Alpine Root and feed it to a SnowHorn. He'll give you a Scarab Bag.
17	Give another root to the SnowHorn, then take control over an ice block.
18	Push the block against a cliff and use it to climb up to another area.
19	Pay a BribeClaw 25 Scarabs for passage into the ThornTail Hollow tunnel.
20	Visit the queen, then go in search of White GrubTubs. Dig into the ancient well.
21	Use a Bomb Spore to blast into a cave. Drop in and earn the Rocket Boost.
22	Break a natural bridge with a spore. Use a piece of the bridge to open a gate.
23	Show a ThornTail that you have a lantern, then blast your way into a dark hole.
24	Use a spore to cut a pillar down to size, then hop across the top of the pillar.
25	Give six White GrubTubs to the queen to earn the SharpClaw Prison Key.
26	Use the Rocket Boost to explore an area over the ThornTail Store.
27	Change the flow of the water for passage back to SnowHorn Wastes.
28	Rocket-Boost up to a locked cage. Open the cage and collect Fuel Cells.
29	Enter the SharpClaw Prison and talk to the SnowHorn in the ice.
30	Save the SnowHorn.
31	After traveling to DarkIce Mines, dig into a building and collect the Shackle Key.
32	Free the shackled SnowHorn. She'll give you a Bridge Cog as a reward.
33	Use the Bridge Cog to operate a mechanism that extends a bridge over a gap.
34	Free a SnowHorn from two SharpClaws. Tricky will learn the Flame Command.
35	Melt an ice barrier in the settlement and search a building for an Alpine Root.
36	Drop into the ravine and melt another barrier to collect a root in a cave.
37	Feed both roots to the SnowHorn and take a ride into the SharpClaw fortress.
38	Melt a cave-blocking ice barrier in the fortress and make your way to the cannon.
39	Take control of the cannon, then fire on SharpClaws and a barrier.
40	Collect three cogs and use them to extend a bridge over the ravine.
41	Light four furnaces within a time limit to open a door. Collect the Dinosaur Horn.
42	Use the horn to call a mammoth. Ride the creature through a storm.
43	When you reach a blocked cave, use the SnowHorn to break through the blockade.
44	Hop onto a Jet Bike. Ride through the ravine and into DarkIce Mines.
45	Hit a Fire Blast Switch to shut off a flame jet. Collect the Silver Prison Cell Key.
46	Use the key to free Tricky, then melt an ice barrier and collect the gold key.
47	Knock three icicles into a pond and use them as platforms to hop across the water.
48	Carry a Fuel Barrel up the path, blast through a barrier at the top and hit the switch.
49	Hit a switch to complete a bridge. Make your way to a SharpClaw cannon.
50	Take control of the cannon and blast two boarded-up switches to trigger a bridge.
51	Warp to Boss Galdon, break the ice and fight the creature for the SpellStone.
52	Back in ThornTail Hollow, hit a burning tree to collect Fire Weeds.
53	Use Fire Weeds and Tricky's Flame Command to light three beacons.
54	Use a Bomb Spore to blast your way into the tunnel to Moon Mountain Pass.
55	Drop into a wind tunnel and float up in another on your way to the pass.
56	As you run through the pass, avoid rolling barrels.
57	Use the Moon Pass Key to open a huge gate, then fight an armored SharpClaw.
58	Hop across a lava pool on three sliding platforms.
59	Wait for a flame to stop burning, then drop into a hole to reach the floor below.
60	Deal with the dangers of Volcano Force Point Temple—barrels and wide gaps.
61	Use the SpellStone to enter the temple proper and light two orbs for admittance.
62	Light fires to make two platforms appear. Cross gaps and earn the Ice Blast.
63	Extinguish flames with the Ice Blast to trigger the appearance of an elevator.
64	Climb a long ladder and extinguish four flames on a ledge to open a door.
65	Cross a fiery gap, turn around and hit a switch to stop moving platforms.
66	When you reach the middle of the temple, put the SpellStone in its place.
67	Use the Rocket Boost and Ice Blast to collect Fuel Cells on a ledge.
68	Talk to a spirit in the pass, explore a cave and earn the Ground Quake upgrade.
69	Use Ground Quake to defeat the first Kalda Chom and collect a MoonSeed.
70	Place the MoonSeed in a planting patch and use fire to make it grow into a vine.
71	Fight crater-dwelling Kalda Choms, collect MoonSeeds and explore the upper pass.
72	After a meteor falls, pick up the small pieces and use them to block steam vents.
73	After you warp to the Krazoa Shrine, swim across a pool and extinguish a flame.
74	Swim across a pool, turn and fire at a switch to raise the water of another pool.
75	Navigate a narrow walkway, crossing fire geysers, turn and hit a Fire Blast Switch.
76	Take the Krazoa Test of Combat. Fight a SharpClaw army within a tight time limit.
77	Return to Moon Mountain Pass and make your way back to ThornTail Hollow.
78	After you warp to Krazoa Palace, fight SharpClaws to open a Life-Force Door.
79	Collect FireFlies, light your way across a dark area and toss a barrel at a barrier.
80	Hit a switch to make flame jets move. Pass the jets and blast a barrier.
81	Light two orbs to weaken a flame-throwing machine, then target the machine.
82	Use wind lifts to rise up to the roof of the palace.
83	Once on the roof, locate Krystal and release the Krazoa Spirit.
84	After you return to the surface, collect a Scarab Bag and pay the Gold Scarab.
85	In Cape Claw, pay a BribeClaw or use the Rocket Boost to go around him.
86	Talk to a dinosaur on the pier to learn about four missing Gold Bars.
87	After you collect the Gold Bars, give them to the dinosaur. He'll drop a ladder.
88	Push blocks over poisonous gas vents to stop the gas flow and open a door.
89	Talk to Queen CloudRunner to learn about the problems in her fortress.
90	After you fly to CloudRunner Fortress, run over an obstacle course on the water.
91	Run up a spiral path, climb down a ladder and hit a switch to open a door.
92	Break out of the prison and sneak past the guard.
93	Blast a hole through the roof. Radio the crew and get the SharpClaw disguise.
94	Use the SharpClaw disguise to fool the guard and collect the staff.
95	Free the prisoners and get the Power Generator Key.
96	Hit a Fire Blast Switch to open a door, then climb a wall to the roof.
97	Hit a switch and extinguish flames as you prepare to collect three Light Gems.
98	Push the left button in the center of the courtyard, then run to the green gem.
99	Push the middle button. Climb boxes to the upper ledge and get the orange gem.
100	Push the right button, run to a pad and Rocket-Boost to collect the blue gem.

101	Use the Generator Key and the Light Gems to bring power to the wind lifts.
102	Use a wind lift to rise to a higher section and fight SharpClaws to open a door.
103	Disguised as a SharpClaw, transport a barrel to a ledge and blow open a path.
104	Hit switches on both sides of the queen's cage to raise the gate.
105	Carry a barrel across a wind lift and use it to destroy the queen's cage.
106	Fight a SharpClaw in the dock area and play the flute to save a CloudRunner child.
107	Jump across a wind lift and fight two SharpClaws to save another child.
108	The third child is on the other side of a wall. Drop down, cross over and boost.
109	The final child is in the dock area. Fight four SharpClaws to rescue it.
110	Throw a barrel into the wind lift, drop it in the treasure room and get the SpellStone.
111	Save a LightFoot from two SharpClaws in Cape Claw and earn a Fire Gem.
112	Climb up the stone and wood ledges and use your disguise to open a door.
113	Make a platform in a flooded room pop up. Hop onto the platform and hit a switch.
114	Extinguish a flame and collect a Fire Gem from a Krazoa Head.
115	Put both Fire Gems in their places and use Tricky to bring light into the room.
116	Hit a switch to flood a room, then push a block onto a plate to open a gate.
117	Have Tricky stay on a plate, then touch tiles to shut off a room's electricity.
118	Navigate narrow walkways and hit a switch to light the colored fire.
119	Walk on another walkway and hit two more switches to shut off the water flow.
120	Solve a color-matching puzzle to light an orb and activate a warp.
121	Hit switches to raise and lower the water level so you can access the next area.
122	Activate a torch turntable and douse the flames by tilting water-filled containers.
123	Slide a block through a maze by hitting it with Fire Blast shots.
124	Rocket-Boost up to a high ledge and explore the duct system.
125	Light an orb to make a bridge appear. Warp to the SpellStone Chamber.
126	Fight LightFoots, in LightFoot Village, with help from a CloudRunner.
127	Find the round carving in the ground, near the village entrance.
128	Look for a thorny blockade on a wall. Burn it away and dig for the square carving.
129	Swim to a patch of land and dig for a triangle carving at the base of a stilted hut.
130	Put all three carvings in place to make platforms appear in the water.
131	Find the leader of the LightFoots and talk to him about their tests.
132	Take the Tracking Test and trigger four totems before time runs out.
133	Push the village strongman, MuscleFoot, into a pit in the Test of Strength.
134	Enter the inner sanctum and complete a spinning-totem puzzle.
135	Shake trees to find three LightFoot children.
136	Explore the forest in the village for another set of triplets.
137	Search for children in the underground area and shoo them out.
138	Use a new Rocket Boost Pad to explore the outer edge of the village.
139	On your way to the Krazoa Test of Fear, run through a long chamber, past flames.
140	Swim through a draining, spike-filled pool to an open door.
141	Run against the flow of rolling barrels to reach a door before it closes.
142	Take the Krazoa Test of Fear and face a huge image of General Scales.
143	After you pass the test, warp to Krazoa Palace and release the spirit.
144	After returning to ThornTail Hollow, save a cluster of eggs from attackers.
145	After you save the eggs, drop into a cave to earn the Portal Device.
146	Use the Portal Device to open the space gate to the Walled City.
147	Use Ground Quake to shake the Sun Beacon tile. Run to the beacon and light it.
148	Shake the tile near the Moon Beacon, then run and light the beacon.
149	Make your way to the underground passage and talk to King EarthWalker.
150	Cross a wooden bridge, burn some brambles and earn the upgraded Ground Quake.
151	Talk to four EarthWalkers near the river and hit switches to light torches.
152	Run and swim through a timed ring race on the river to enter a small structure.
153	Enter the structure in the ravine to find the Silver Tooth.
154	Defeat all RedEyes to dissolve a Life-Force Door and collect the Gold Tooth.
155	Use the Silver and Gold Teeth to enter the boss arena and battle Boss RedEye.
156	Return to Volcano Force Point Temple and open a new path.

157	Cross a lava pool by extinguishing flames and hopping onto moving platforms.
158	Extinguish flames in a specific order to open a door.
159	Have Tricky stay on a pressure plate to access a switch.
160	Light three orbs by firing through flames from a moving platform.
161	Warp to the center of the temple and put the SpellStone in its place.
162	Return to ThornTail Hollow, where you'll find dinosaurs under attack. Save them.
163	Collect the Large Scarab Bag, then find Scarabs and buy the SnowHorn Artifact.
164	Return the SnowHorn Artifact to its owner and run through an obstacle course.
165	After you clear the obstacle course, warp to the shrine for a test.
166	Carry a Fuel Barrel on a narrow, windy path and use it to break through a barrier.
167	As you transport a Fuel Barrel across a pool, hit a switch to redirect flames.
168	Toss the barrel across a wind tunnel, then carry it and throw it into a barrier.
169	Take the Krazoa Test of Strength and push a giant stone turntable.
170	Warp to the Krazoa Palace and release the Krazoa Spirit.
171	Return to ThornTail Hollow and talk to a ThornTail to open the gate to Dragon Roc
172	Before you leave, make sure that you have purchased the Hi-Def Display Device.
173	After you land on Dragon Rock, climb the large building while avoiding the flame
174	Transport a barrel along the high ledge, then blast your way into the building.
175	Avoid spinning flames and hit a switch to free an EarthWalker.
176	Ride the EarthWalker and charge into four rock-embedded Power Generators.
177	Explore a new part of the huge building and save a High Top.
178	After you ride the HighTop, enter a new area and search for a CloudRunner.
179	Direct a barrel carrier to take a barrel to a high ledge and shut off flame jets.
180	Hit a switch to make the CloudRunner's cage move, then burn the cord.
181	After you destroy four spires, take on Boss Drakor in the tower.
182	Return to Cape Claw, take over the cannon and blast open the temple entrance
183	Hit a giant rock on the beach to break into a staff-energy upgrade cave.
184	Have Tricky stay on a pressure plate, then turn off the power to a series of tiles
185	Use the warp to return to the lower levels of the Ocean Force Point Temple.
186	Use blocks to climb up to a high switch.
187	Use the SharpClaw disguise to reveal a switch, then hit it to raise the water le
188	Extinguish the flames on the turntable by tipping color-matching water contain
189	Push the large block through the maze by hitting it with Fire Blast shots.
190	Rocket up to the high ledge and make your way to the Warp Pad.
191	Warp to the middle of the temple and put the last SpellStone in place.
192	Return to the Walled City and talk to King EarthWalker in front of the temple.
193	Push blocks in the courtyard of the Sun Temple to open an iris on the roof.
194	Use the Hi-Def Display Device to zoom through the iris. A door will open.
195	Move blocks into place so their faces show and reveal a maze.
196	Hit switches in the maze to make sections of the wall disappear.
197	Hit a series of switches to earn the Sun Stone.
198	Move blocks in the Moon Temple courtyard and zoom through an iris to enter
199	Hit a switch to make gates drop and rise, then run over falling tiles to a door
200	Use Ground Quake on a floor panel, then navigate an invisible maze.
201	Fire through holes in a spinning disk to hit Fire Blast Switches. Get the Moo
202	Put the stones in their rightful places, then warp to the Krazoa Shrine.
203	In the shrine, fly through wind currents and avoid a series of flame jets.
204	Extinguish flames on a narrow walkway and advance to an open gate.
205	Fly to platforms with spinning flames. Avoid the fiery blasts.
206	Take the Krazoa Test of Knowledge and match items with their places of ori
207	Fly to the roof of Krazoa Palace, drop down to a high floor and release the s
208	Return to the roof and warp to a room with a large stage in the center.
209	Face off with General Scales and collect the final spirit.

STOP After you release the last Krazoa Spirit, you will learn more about the
of the trouble on Dinosaur Planet, then you will embark on a final flight for a spa
tle against the tyrant of the Lylat System, Andross.